Oracle

MW01283341

Study Guide for

1Z0-051: Oracle Database 11g:

SQL Fundamentals I

Matthew Morris

**Study Guide for Oracle Database 11g: SQL Fundamentals I
(Exam 1Z0-051)**

ISBN-13: 978-1475204667
ISBN-10: 1475204663

Table of Contents

What to Expect from the Test

The test consists of 70 multiple choice or multiple answer questions. The passing score listed on Oracle Education at this time is 60%, but as with all Oracle certification tests, they note it is subject to change. This test contains a higher number of exhibits than the average for Oracle certification exams. A significant percentage of the questions will involve recognizing whether or not a given SQL statement will execute without error. You'll be asked to identify the SQL statement or statements that perform a given task. Generally some of the alternatives contain errors, and you'll need to be able to recognize this.

To do well on the test you have to have a good grasp of SQL syntax rules. You'll also need to be able to utilize some common SQL functions, recognize the result of basic DDL operations, and know some of the facts regarding how SQL statements and functions are executed. Not all of the exhibits in the test are really crucial to answering the question being asked. You should read the question being asked before viewing the exhibit. If nothing else, reading the question first will provide you with information on what to look for in the exhibit, and it may allow you to skip viewing it entirely, giving you more time for other questions. Be sure to look at all of the answers. In some cases, more than one answer could be considered 'correct', but one of the two is a better answer. Also, it's valuable to look through the questions that contain SQL statements to find those with errors. Once you have eliminated those with obvious errors, you can concentrate on the remaining options to find the best solution.

What to Expect from this Study Guide

This document is built around the subject matter topics that Oracle Education has indicated will be tested. I've gathered together material from several Oracle documentation sources along with results from numerous SQL queries similar to what you'll see on the test. The guide covers a significant percentage of the information and operations that you must be familiar with in order to pass the test.

What this guide is intended to do is to present the information that will be covered on the exam at the level it will likely be asked. The guide assumes that you have at least a rudimentary knowledge of SQL. While the guide works from basic principles of SQL, no book in and of itself is a substitute for hands-on experience. You need to have spent time writing queries, running them, and seeing the result before scheduling this test. Since Oracle has made the Oracle XE version of its database free to download and use, there is no reason why anyone who wants to learn to use Oracle cannot get hands-on experience.

The goal of this guide is to present to you the concepts and information most likely to be the subject of test questions, and to do so in a very compact format that will allow you to read through it more than once to reinforce the information. If much of the information presented in this guide is completely new to you then you need to supplement this guide with other source of study materials to build a firm foundation of Oracle SQL knowledge. If you have a reasonable grounding in the basic concepts and are comfortable writing basic SQL statements, then this book will supply you with the facts you need to pass the exam and improve your skills as a SQL developer. If you don't have any experience with SQL at all, the compressed format of this guide is not likely to be the best method for learning. It may provide you with the information you need to pass the test, but you're likely to have deficiencies as a SQL Developer.

Retrieving Data Using the SQL SELECT Statement

A query is a database operation that retrieves rows from one or more tables or views. In this context, a top-level SELECT statement is called a query. If there is a second SELECT nested within the first, it is called a subquery. Essentially all operations that pull data out of a table in an Oracle database have a SELECT command involved at some level.

List the capabilities of SQL SELECT statements

SELECT statements are used to retrieve information from database tables. When a SELECT statement retrieves data, it can do the following three types of work:

- **Selection** -- You can filter the SELECT statement to choose only the rows that you want to be returned.
- **Projection** -- You can choose only the columns that you want to be returned by your query, or create new information through the use of expressions.
- **Joining** -- You can use the SQL JOIN operators to link two or more tables to allow you to return data that is stored in more than one table.

The syntax of a minimal SELECT statement in Oracle is:

```
SELECT select_list
FROM   table_reference;
```

These four elements exist in every SELECT statement issued to Oracle (or at least every one that completes successfully). The elements that make up the **select_list** might be columns, functions, literals, etc. The **table_reference** might be an Oracle table, remote table, external table, view, pipelined function, etc. Regardless of the specifics, they must be valid references and be present in the SELECT syntax.

There are a number of words that will be associated with SQL statements throughout the text:

- **Alias** – Aliases are used to provide an alternate (usually shorter or more readable) name for an item in the select list or for a table reference. Aliases improve readability of the statement and are required for certain operations.
- **Keyword** – Keywords are defined individual elements of a SQL statement (SELECT, FROM, WHERE, GROUP BY, etc.)
- **Clause** – A clause is a subset of a SQL statement that is tied to a keyword. For example, "SELECT first_name, last_name" is a SELECT clause.
- **Expression** – An expression is an element in a select list that is not a column. It may or may not contain a column. For example, given the clause "SELECT last_name, first_name, first_name || ' ' || last_name", two elements in the clause (first_name and last_name) are columns, and (first_name || ' ' || last_name) is an expression.
- **Literal** – An element in the SELECT list that will be returned from the query unchanged. For example, "SELECT 'Fred' FROM dual;' would return the text literal 'Fred'.
- **Statement** – A statement is a combination of two or more clauses that form a complete SQL operation. At the bare minimum a SQL statement must include a SELECT clause and a FROM clause.

The DUAL table

The DUAL table in Oracle is a one-column, one row table that is very useful when there is a need to perform an Oracle SQL function that requires a single result that is unrelated to data stored in a user table. The one column in DUAL is called 'DUMMY' and the value in the column for the single row is 'X'. Neither is really important, however, as the table isn't used for what it contains, but for what it does. When making a call to DUAL, the SQL statement contains an operation that needs to be performed. The DUAL table simply acts as a springboard against which to direct the SQL operation so that Oracle can process it and return the results to the user. For example, the following operation returns the current operating system date of the server on which Oracle is installed:

```
SELECT SYSDATE
FROM    dual;

SYSDATE
---------
03-APR-12
```

Throughout this guide, you'll see similar calls to the dual table to perform various SQL operations. The DUAL table is **never** modified and always contains a single row.

SYSDATE vs CURRENT_DATE

In the above example, we used a query against the dual table to call the SYSDATE function. SYSDATE returns the current date and time of the server on which the Oracle database is running. There is a second function called CURRENT_DATE that has a similar capability. The CURRENT_DATE function, however, pulls the current date in the time zone of the database session which makes the call. This may or may not match with the value from SYSDATE. In the example below the two match exactly because the session and server are in the same time zone.

```
SELECT TO_CHAR(SYSDATE, 'DD-MON-YY HH:MI AM') SYS_DATE,
       TO_CHAR(CURRENT_DATE, 'DD-MON-YY HH:MI AM') CURR_DATE
FROM dual;

SYS_DATE                         CURR_DATE
------------------------------   ---------------------------
11-APR-12 11:27 PM               11-APR-12 11:27 PM
```

If the session time zone were altered, the two would return different results:

```
ALTER SESSION SET TIME_ZONE='Europe/Zurich';
session SET altered.
```

```
SELECT TO_CHAR(SYSDATE, 'DD-MON-YY HH:MI AM') SYS_DATE,
       TO_CHAR(CURRENT_DATE, 'DD-MON-YY HH:MI AM') CURR_DATE
FROM dual;

SYS_DATE                    CURR_DATE
-------------------------   -------------------------
11-APR-12 11:27 PM          12-APR-12 05:27 AM
```

Lexical Conventions

The Oracle SQL parser treats single spaces, multiple spaces, and tabs interchangeably. That is to say it doesn't matter when writing SQL if you use one space or fifty, or a tab instead of a space. A single carriage return can be used in lieu of a space in most cases (although two carriage returns together signal the end of a SQL statement). Separating an expression or a comparison operation with a carriage return is not allowed. The following SQL statements would be treated identically by the Oracle SQL Parser:

```
SELECT emp_last,emp_first,salary/2080 FROM employees
WHERE emp_job='Pilot' ORDER BY salary;

SELECT emp_last, emp_first, salary / 2080
FROM    employees
WHERE   emp_job = 'Pilot'
ORDER BY salary;

SELECT emp_last,
       emp_first,
       salary / 2080
FROM    employees
WHERE   emp_job = 'Pilot'
ORDER BY salary;

SELECT
emp_last,
emp_first,
salary / 2080
FROM
employees
WHERE
emp_job = 'Pilot'
ORDER BY
salary;
```

SQL Statements are not case-sensitive with the exception of quoted elements. The following statement is equivalent to the ones above. Changing the case of the quoted element 'Pilot', however, would alter the results of the SQL statement. Note that SINGLE quotes are used to enclose character literals in SQL statements. DOUBLE quotes in SQL statements are used to enclose names used by the Oracle SQL parser (column names, column aliases, table names, table aliases, etc.)

```
select EMP_LAST, EMP_FIRST, SALARY / 2080
from   EMPLOYEES
where  EMP_JOB = 'Pilot'
order by SALARY;
```

Keywords cannot be split across lines, abbreviated, or run together with the rest of their clause without a separator. The separation can be a space, tab, or carriage return, but it must be present. The following three statements would generate an error for each of the three reasons supplied above respectively.

```
SELECT emp_last, emp_first, salary/2080
FROM   employees
WHERE  emp_job='Pilot' ORD
ER BY    salary;
```

```
SEL    emp_last, emp_first, salary/2080
FRM    employees
WHR    emp_job='Pilot'
ORD BY salary;
```

```
SELECTemp_last,emp_first,salary/2080FROMemployees
WHEREemp_job='Pilot'ORDER BYsalary;
```

SQL Statements that will be persistent (i.e. part of a script or procedures as opposed to a single-use ad-hoc query), should be formatted for readability. The use of indentation and selective capitalization will make SQL statements, especially large and complex ones, much easier to read and maintain.

Arithmetic Operators & Precedence

Arithmetic operators can be used with one or two arguments to add, subtract, multiply, and divide numeric values. The addition and subtraction operators can also be used in datetime and interval arithmetic. The arguments used must resolve to numeric data types or to a data type that can be implicitly converted to a numeric type (datetime data types meet this requirement because they are stored internally by Oracle as a numeric value).

You can perform math operations directly via a SQL statement:

```
SELECT 4+4
FROM dual;

4+4
---
  8
```

You can use arithmetic operators to modify table data:

```
SELECT emp_last, emp_first, salary, salary * 1.05
SAL_WITH_RAISE
FROM    employees
WHERE   emp_job = 'Pilot'
ORDER BY salary DESC;
```

EMP_LAST	EMP_FIRST	SALARY	SAL_WITH_RAISE
McCoy	Phil	105000	110250
Thomas	James	98500	103425
Jones	John	97500	102375
Kia	Noh	92250	96862.5
Gun	Top	91500	96075
Skytalker	Luke	90000	94500
Aptop	Dell	87500	91875
Picard	John	49500	51975

Likewise date literals can be manipulated directly via SQL using arithmetic operators, or date values in a table altered:

```
SELECT SYSDATE, SYSDATE+4
FROM dual;

SYSDATE    SYSDATE+4
---------  ---------
27-MAR-12 31-MAR-12


SELECT emp_last, emp_first, start_date, start_date + 60
FROM    employees
WHERE   emp_job = 'Pilot'
ORDER BY start_date;

EMP_LAST    EMP_FIRST   START_DATE START_DATE+60
----------  ----------  ---------- -------------
Jones       John        10-APR-95  09-JUN-95
McCoy       Phil        09-JUN-96  08-AUG-96
Gun         Top         13-OCT-96  12-DEC-96
Thomas      James       12-MAY-99  11-JUL-99
Picard      John        11-NOV-01  10-JAN-02
Skytalker   Luke        10-SEP-02  09-NOV-02
Aptop       Dell        22-AUG-03  21-OCT-03
Kia         Noh         07-JUL-04  05-SEP-04
```

Precedence is the order in which different operators in the same expression are evaluated. Oracle evaluates operators with higher precedence before evaluating those with lower precedence. If there are operators with equal precedence, they are evaluated from left to right within the expression. The plus and minus signs can be used in either a unary fashion or a binary fashion depending on whether they are applied to one or two operands. For example, in '-1', the negative sign is acting as a unary operator and evaluates to 'negative one'. By contrast, in '4 - 1' the negative sign is acting as a binary operator and evaluates to 'four minus one'. The arithmetic operators and their precedence follow:

1. **+, - (as unary operators)** -- Identity, negation,
2. ***, /** -- Multiplication, division
3. **+, - (as binary operators)** -- Addition, subtraction

```
SELECT 3 + 2 * 4
FROM dual;

3+2*4
-----
   11
```

Parentheses can be used to change the order in which the operators are evaluated. When parentheses are nested, the most deeply nested operators are evaluated first:

```
SELECT (3 + 2) * 4
FROM dual;

(3+2)*4
-------
     20
```

When a negative is used as a unary operator, it takes precedence over multiplication or division:

```
SELECT -2 * 6
FROM dual;

-2*6
----
 -12
```

String Concatenation

Arithmetic operators cannot be used with character data. However, it is possible to combine two or more strings together using the concatenation operator. The concatenation operator in Oracle is two vertical bars '||'. When placed between two character expressions, it results in a single combined character column.

```
SELECT emp_first, emp_last,
       emp_first || ' ' || emp_last FIRST_LAST,
       emp_last || ', ' || emp_first LAST_FIRST
FROM   employees
WHERE  emp_job = 'CEO';

EMP_FIRST  EMP_LAST    FIRST _LAST LAS _FIRST
---------- ----------  ----------- ----------
Big        Boss        Big Boss    Boss, Big
```

String concatenation can also be performed by the CONCAT SQL function. The CONCAT function can be used to concatenate two string functions in the same way that the '||' operator works. CONCAT is limited to two values. I don't know of any good reason to use it over the '||' operator, but you may be expected to know about the function on the exam. Below is an example of how the previous SQL statement could have been written using CONCAT. Since CONCAT can only join two strings at a time, the function must be used twice on each of the two expressions being concatenated.

```
SELECT  emp_first, emp_last,
        CONCAT(CONCAT(emp_first, ' '), emp_last)
            AS FIRST_LAST,
        CONCAT(CONCAT(emp_last, ', '), emp_first)
            AS LAST_FIRST
FROM    employees
WHERE   emp_job = 'CEO';

EMP_FIRST   EMP_LAST    FIRST_LAST    LAST_FIRST
----------  ----------  ------------  ------------
Big         Boss        Big Boss      Boss, Big
```

Column Aliases

The default heading returned for columns selected in a query is simply the column name itself, or if an expression, the text of the expression with spaces removed. For a SELECT it may be desirable to provide a cleaner, shorter, or more descriptive heading for the results. For some SQL operations, providing an alias for expressions is a requirement. To specify an alias for a column or expression, you can provide the alias immediately after the column name, separated by a space. You can also use the optional 'AS' keyword when specifying an alias. The AS keyword makes SQL more readable, especially for long statements. By default, aliases are returned in upper-case and cannot have spaces or special characters. You can bypass that behavior by enclosing the alias in double-quotation marks. The four examples below show the same SQL statement using no alias, two alternate syntaxes for aliasing columns and the use of an alias enclosed by double quotes.

```
SELECT  emp_first, emp_last,
        emp_first || ' ' || emp_last
FROM    employees
WHERE   emp_job = 'CEO';
```

```
EMP_FIRST   EMP_LAST    EMP_FIRST||''||EMP_LAST
----------  ----------  ------------------------
Big         Boss        Big Boss


SELECT emp_first, emp_last,
       emp_first || ' ' || emp_last full_name
FROM   employees
WHERE  emp_job = 'CEO';


EMP_FIRST   EMP_LAST    FULL_NAME
----------  ----------  ----------------------
Big         Boss        Big Boss


SELECT emp_first, emp_last,
       emp_first || ' ' || emp_last AS full_name
FROM   employees
WHERE  emp_job = 'CEO';


EMP_FIRST   EMP_LAST    FULL_NAME
----------  ----------  ----------------------
Big         Boss        Big Boss


SELECT emp_first, emp_last,
       emp_first || ' ' || emp_last AS "Full Name"
FROM   employees
WHERE  emp_job = 'CEO';


EMP_FIRST   EMP_LAST    Full Name
----------  ----------  ----------------------
Big         Boss        Big Boss
```

Handling character data containing quotes

Character literals that are included in a SELECT list must be enclosed in single-quotes. When the character data includes one or more single-quotes within it, they conflict with the enclosing quotes and generate Oracle errors. Prior to Oracle 9i, this was normally handled by replacing any single quote operators in text literals with two together (i.e. replace {'} with {''}). Putting two single-quotes together within a quote string resolves to a single quote when parsed. This method works, but is fairly cumbersome if lots of data is involved. With 9i, Oracle introduced the alternative quote operator. This allows you to change the character to be used to enclose character data. If you wanted to use curly brackets as the delimiter, the syntax would be q'{ string_literal }'. An example of a string literal that is causing an error is below:

```
SELECT emp_first || ''s plane is a ' || act_name
FROM   aircraft_types act
       NATURAL JOIN aircraft_fleet
       NATURAL JOIN employees;

Error starting at line 1 in command:
SELECT emp_first || ''s plane is a ' || act_name
FROM   aircraft_types act
       NATURAL JOIN aircraft_fleet
       NATURAL JOIN employees;

Error at Command Line:1 Column:24
Error report:
SQL Error: ORA-00923: FROM keyword not found where expected
00923. 00000 -  "FROM keyword not found where expected"
*Cause:
*Action:
```

The statement updated to utilize the alternate quote operator to employ parentheses for the delimiter would be:

```
SELECT emp_first || q'('s plane is a )' || act_name
FROM   aircraft_types act
       NATURAL JOIN aircraft_fleet
       NATURAL JOIN employees;

EMP_FIRST||Q'('SPLANEISA)'||ACT_NAME
-----------------------------------
John's plane is a Boeing 767
Top's plane is a Boeing 767
Phil's plane is a Boeing 737
James's plane is a Boeing 757
John's plane is a Boeing 747
Luke's plane is a Boeing 747
Dell's plane is a Boeing 747
Noh's plane is a Boeing 767
```

The delimiter can be any single character desired, or it you can make use of any of the paired characters: <>, (), {}, or [].

NULL Values

The NULL value is something that is often misunderstood by people new to Oracle. When a column or variable in Oracle is NULL, it has no value. This is not the same as a having a value of zero or having a value of a blank space. The 'Zero' and 'Space' characters are still data – they have a value. A column with a value of 'zero' is equal to all other columns with a value of zero and the same is true of a column that has a single blank space. However, a column that contains a NULL value doesn't equal anything. In Oracle, NULL does not equal NULL. This sounds strange, but essentially when a column is NULL, it means "I don't know what the value is." If you don't know what the value of Row A is, and you don't know what the value of row B is, are the two equal? The answer is – you don't know. The upshot is, that if you query for rows in a table using the condition "WHERE column_name = NULL", you will never get any results:

```
SELECT afl_id, emp_first, emp_last
FROM    employees
WHERE   afl_id = NULL;

no rows selected
```

However, if you use the condition WHERE column_name IS NULL, you will have much greater success. The IS NULL operator is designed specifically to evaluate to TRUE for values that are NULL.

```
SELECT afl_id, emp_first, emp_last
FROM    employees
WHERE   afl_id IS NULL;

AFL_ID EMP_FIRST  EMP_LAST
------ ---------- ----------
       Big        Boss
       Adam       Smith
       Rick       Jameson
       Rob        Stoner
       Bill       Abong
       Janet      Jeckson
       Alf        Alien
       Norm       Storm
       Fred       Stoneflint
```

NULL values are also extremely contagious when combined with other non-NULL data. When any non-NULL value is combined with a NULL value using a mathematical operator, the result is NULL:

```
SELECT 2 + NULL, 2 - NULL, 2 * NULL, 2 / NULL
FROM   dual;

2+NULL 2-NULL 2*NULL 2/NULL
------ ------ ------ ------
```

However, concatenating a NULL to a character string will simply mean that the string is unchanged:

```
SELECT 'Fred' || NULL, 'Wilma' || NULL || 'Barney'
FROM   dual;

'FRED'||NULL 'WILMA'||NULL||'BARNEY'
------------ ----------------------
Fred         WilmaBarney
```

In addition to retrieving and manipulating data that exists in database tables, a SELECT statement can return results that are not stored in tables. There are several ways this can be done.

Expressions

Expressions in the select list of a SQL statement include essentially everything except a bare column name. They could be literals, column data that has been modified by operators, or SQL functions.

- **Text Literals** -- Use to specify values whenever 'string' appears in the syntax of expressions, conditions, SQL functions, and SQL statements. Text literals are always surrounded by single quotation marks.

```
SELECT 'Fred' AS STRING_LIT
FROM dual;
STRING_LIT
----------
Fred
```

Text literals can be used to provide context or formatting to the data being selected from the table.

```
SELECT emp_last || ', ' || emp_first || ' (' || emp_job ||
       ') started on ' || start_date AS EMP_BIO
FROM   employees
WHERE  emp_job = 'Pilot';

EMP_BIO
--------------------------------------------------
Jones, John (Pilot) started on 10-APR-95
Gun, Top (Pilot) started on 13-OCT-96
McCoy, Phil (Pilot) started on 09-JUN-96
Thomas, James (Pilot) started on 12-MAY-99
Picard, John (Pilot) started on 11-NOV-01
Skytalker, Luke (Pilot) started on 10-SEP-02
Aptop, Dell (Pilot) started on 22-AUG-03
Kia, Noh (Pilot) started on 07-JUL-04
```

- **Numeric Literals** -- Use numeric literal notation to specify fixed and floating-point numbers.

```
SELECT 14.5 AS NUM_LIT
FROM dual;

NUM_LIT
-------
14.5
```

- **Datetime Literals** -- You can specify a date value as a string literal, or you can convert a character or numeric value to a date value using the TO_DATE function.

```
SELECT '10-JAN-12' AS STRING_LIT,
       TO_DATE('01/10/2012', 'MM/DD/YYYY') AS TD_LIT
FROM dual;

STRING_LIT TD_LIT
---------- ---------
10-JAN-12  10-JAN-12
```

In the above statement, the second column was explicitly converted to a date data type, but the value returned by SQL*Plus looks exactly like the string in the first column. This is because Oracle doesn't ever display dates as they are stored in the database. What Oracle actually stores in a

DATE field behind the scenes is a numeric value. Whenever a data is displayed as the result of a SELECT operation, Oracle automatically converts it to a character value. The default date format for this is 'DD-MON-YY', but this can be altered by setting the NLS_DATE_FORMAT session parameter.

SQL Functions

The use of SQL functions can also generate results that are not stored in database tables. SQL functions will be discussed in more depth in a later section.

Pseudocolumns

A pseudocolumn in Oracle in many ways behaves like a regular table column, but is not actually stored in the database. They can be referenced by SELECT statements, but they cannot be inserted, updated or deleted. Pseudocolumns are similar to a function without arguments in how they act. The two pseudocolumns that exist for all SQL statements are listed below. There are others that exist for specific SQL operations.

- **ROWNUM** -- For each row returned by a query, this pseudocolumn returns a number indicating the order in which Oracle returns the row.
- **ROWID** -- For each row in the database, this pseudocolumn returns the address of the row.

Displaying the Structure of a Table

Both the Oracle SQL*Plus and SQL Developer tools support the DESCRIBE command. This command is used to display the structure of a table. The syntax is either "DESCRIBE table_name' or the command can be abbreviated as 'DESC table_name'. The results will show all columns in the table, their data types and size (where appropriate) and whether or not the columns have a NOT NULL constraint.

```
DESCRIBE employees

Name            Null      Type
--------------- --------- ------------
EMP_ID          NOT NULL  NUMBER
AFL_ID                    NUMBER
EMP_FIRST                 VARCHAR2(10)
EMP_LAST        NOT NULL  VARCHAR2(10)
EMP_JOB                   VARCHAR2(10)
EMP_SUPERVISOR            NUMBER
SALARY                    NUMBER
START_DATE                DATE
```

Execute a basic SELECT statement

The most basic SELECT statement consists of the SELECT keyword, a list of one or more columns or expressions (referred to as the select_list), the FROM keyword, and a table or view (referred to as the table_reference).

```
SELECT apt_id, apt_name, apt_abbr
FROM   airports;

APT_ID APT_NAME                        APT_ABBR
------ ------------------------------- --------
     1 Orlando, FL                     MCO
     2 Atlanta, GA                     ATL
     3 Miami, FL                       MIA
     4 Jacksonville, FL                JAX
     5 Dallas/Fort Worth               DFW
```

If you wish to display all columns from a table, rather than entering each column into the SELECT clause, you can use the asterisk wildcard. The asterisk will return the complete set of columns (excluding pseudocolumns) from the table (or tables) listed in the FROM clause. If a query contains multiple tables, you can prefix the asterisk with a table name or table alias to return all columns from just one of the tables in the query.

When the asterisk is used in a SELECT, the columns will be returned by the SELECT operation in the order indicated by the COLUMN_ID column of the *_TAB_COLUMNS data dictionary view for the table reference. The column headings will be the upper-case column names (there is no way to use the asterisk *and* supply column aliases.

```
SELECT  *
FROM    airports;

APT_ID APT_NAME                       APT_ABBR
------ ------------------------------ --------
     1 Orlando, FL                    MCO
     2 Atlanta, GA                    ATL
     3 Miami, FL                      MIA
     4 Jacksonville, FL               JAX
     5 Dallas/Fort Worth              DFW
```

Restricting and Sorting Data

The ability to retrieve specific information from a database is possibly the most important aspect of SQL. Limiting the rows being returned and defining the order they should be returned in are both significant parts of that functionality.

Limit the rows that are retrieved by a query

DISTINCT | UNIQUE

One of the ways in which to limit the amount of data returned by a query it to display only one result when the table(s) being queried have multiple copies of duplicate data. This can be done using either the DISTINCT or UNIQUE keywords. The DISTINCT keyword is much more commonly used than the UNIQUE keyword, but either will perform the same function. When a row contains matching values for **every** expression in the select list, the DISTINCT/UNIQUE keyword will only return a single row. It is not possible to use DISTINCT/UNIQUE if one or more of the expressions being returned is a LOB column. The two statements below show the effect of adding the DISTINCT keyword to a query.

```
SELECT act_body_style, act_decks
FROM   aircraft_types;

ACT_BODY_STYLE ACT_DECKS
-------------- ----------
Wide           Double
Wide           Single
Narrow         Single
Narrow         Single


SELECT DISTINCT act_body_style, act_decks
FROM   aircraft_types;

ACT_BODY_STYLE ACT_DECKS
-------------- ----------
Wide           Single
Wide           Double
Narrow         Single
```

In the second example, the duplicated rows from the first query with a body style of narrow and a single deck have been reduced to a single row. The DISTINCT query still has two rows with a wide body style and two rows with a single deck, but no rows where <u>every</u> column value is identical.

WHERE Clause

The WHERE clause of SQL statements allows you to create conditions that rows must meet in order to be returned by the query. The conditions in the clause may be extremely simple or mind-numbingly complex. If you omit the WHERE clause, all rows of the table or tables in the query will be returned by the SQL (although the use of DISTINCT/UNIQUE would cause only the unique results to be displayed). If columns are aliased in the SELECT clause, the aliases cannot be used to reference columns in the WHERE clause.

When text or date literals are included in the where clause, they must be enclosed in single quotes. If a date literal is being compared to a date data type in a table, the literal has to be converted to a DATE data type as well. If the string value is supplied in the same format as the default session format, then Oracle can perform an implicit data conversion. If it is not, you must use explicitly convert the value to the date data type. Date and character conversions will be covered later in this guide. When a text literal is being compared to a text column, the comparison is always case-specific.

The most common comparison operators for a WHERE clause are:
- = -- Equal to
- < -- Less than
- > -- Greater than
- <= -- Less than or equal to
- >= -- Greater than or equal to
- <> -- Greater than or Less than
- !=, ^= -- Not equal to
- **IN(set)** – Value contained within set
- **BETWEEN val1 AND val2** – Between val1 and val2 (inclusive)
- **LIKE** – Matches a given pattern that can include wildcards

- **IS NULL** – Is a NULL value
- **IS NOT NULL** – Is a non-NULL value

The equality operator is almost assuredly the most common condition applied to filter the data being returned from a SQL query. In the example below the query will return only those rows of the AIRCRAFT_TYPES table where the ACT_DECKS is equal to the text 'Single'.

```
SELECT *
FROM    aircraft_types
WHERE   act_decks = 'Single';

ACT_ID ACT_NAME      ACT_BODY_STYLE ACT_DECKS  ACT_SEATS
------ ------------- -------------- ---------- ---------
     2 Boeing 767    Wide           Single           350
     3 Boeing 737    Narrow         Single           200
     4 Boeing 757    Narrow         Single           240
```

The results of the above query can be completely reversed by using the not-equals operator '!='. This operator (or the alternate 'not equal' operator '^=') is interchangeable with the Greater than/Less than operator '<>'.

```
SELECT *
FROM    aircraft_types
WHERE   act_decks != 'Single';

ACT_ID ACT_NAME      ACT_BODY_STYLE ACT_DECKS  ACT_SEATS
------ ------------- -------------- ---------- ---------
     1 Boeing 747    Wide           Double           416
```

The example below makes use of the less-than sign '<' for filtering the results:

```
SELECT *
FROM    aircraft_types
WHERE   act_seats < 416;

ACT_ID ACT_NAME      ACT_BODY_STYLE ACT_DECKS  ACT_SEATS
------ ------------- -------------- ---------- ---------
     2 Boeing 767    Wide           Single           350
     3 Boeing 737    Narrow         Single           200
     4 Boeing 757    Narrow         Single           240
```

The example below makes use of the IN operator for filtering the results:

```
SELECT  *
FROM    aircraft_types
WHERE   act_name IN ('Boeing 737', 'Boeing 767');

ACT_ID ACT_NAME     ACT_BODY_STYLE ACT_DECKS  ACT_SEATS
------ ------------ -------------- ---------- ---------
     2 Boeing 767   Wide           Single           350
     3 Boeing 737   Narrow         Single           200
```

The example below makes use of the BETWEEN operator for filtering the results. Note that the BETWEEN is inclusive because the endpoints of 200 and 240 are included in the results. If the BETWEEN operator were NOT inclusive, the range would need to have been 199 -> 241.

```
SELECT  *
FROM    aircraft_types
WHERE   act_seats BETWEEN 200
                  AND 240;

ACT_ID ACT_NAME     ACT_BODY_STYLE ACT_DECKS  ACT_SEATS
------ ------------ -------------- ---------- ---------
     3 Boeing 737   Narrow         Single           200
     4 Boeing 757   Narrow         Single           240
```

The example below shows pattern matching using the LIKE operator. The % wildcard looks for zero or more occurrences of any character or combination of characters, whereas the _ wildcard looks for a single indeterminate character. The condition below then will return any aircraft where the number '5' is the second-to-last character in the string.

```
SELECT  *
FROM    aircraft_types
WHERE   act_name LIKE '%5_';

ACT_ID ACT_NAME     ACT_BODY_STYLE ACT_DECKS  ACT_SEATS
------ ------------ -------------- ---------- ---------
     4 Boeing 757   Narrow         Single           240
```

Combining two or more conditions with Logical Operators

There are three logical operators that can be used in conjunction with operators in a WHERE clause to generate more complex (and specific) logic for identifying rows:

- **AND** – Evaluates to TRUE if the components on both sides are TRUE.
- **OR** -- Evaluates to TRUE if the component on either side are TRUE.
- **NOT** – Evaluates to TRUE if the identified component is FALSE

When two or more conditions in a WHERE clause are combined (or reversed) through the use of logical operators, results are returned by the query only when the complete clause evaluates to TRUE. The following two examples make use of two conditions each, the first combined with the 'AND' operator and the second with the 'OR' operator. In the first statement, both conditions have to evaluate to TRUE for a row to be returned. In the second, a row is returned if either condition evaluates to TRUE.

```
SELECT *
FROM    aircraft_types
WHERE   act_seats < 416
AND     act_body_style = 'Narrow';
```

ACT_ID	ACT_NAME	ACT_BODY_STYLE	ACT_DECKS	ACT_SEATS
3	Boeing 737	Narrow	Single	200
4	Boeing 757	Narrow	Single	240

```
SELECT *
FROM    aircraft_types
WHERE   act_seats < 220
OR      act_decks = 'Double';
```

ACT_ID	ACT_NAME	ACT_BODY_STYLE	ACT_DECKS	ACT_SEATS
1	Boeing 747	Wide	Double	416
3	Boeing 737	Narrow	Single	200

If a WHERE clause contains a combination of both 'AND' and 'OR' operators, it's very likely that the conditions must be combined within parentheses for the desired results to be achieved. In the below example, the first condition excludes planes with more than one deck (the 747). This is AND'ed with the second condition that filters out planes with a wide body style deck (excluding the 747 and 767). The final condition is OR'd in and provides an exception for planes with more than 200 seats.

The intent of the final condition is to include the 767 but exclude the 747 (the logic being to have one deck and either a narrow body or greater than 200 seats). However, the result of the query has all four aircraft types. The reason for this is that the OR operator has equal precedence with the AND operator. The conditions are being evaluated from the top down.

```
SELECT  *
FROM    aircraft_types
WHERE   act_decks = 'Single'
AND     act_body_style != 'Wide'
OR      act_seats > 200;
```

ACT_ID	ACT_NAME	ACT_BODY_STYLE	ACT_DECKS	ACT_SEATS
1	Boeing 747	Wide	Double	416
2	Boeing 767	Wide	Single	350
3	Boeing 737	Narrow	Single	200
4	Boeing 757	Narrow	Single	240

To return the 767 and not the 747, the second and third conditions must be evaluated together and then the result ANDed to the first condition. To do this, the conditions must be enclosed by parentheses to change the order of evaluation. The query below returns the intended results:

```
SELECT  *
FROM    aircraft_types
WHERE   act_decks = 'Single'
AND     (   act_body_style != 'Wide'
        OR  act_seats > 200);
```

ACT_ID	ACT_NAME	ACT_BODY_STYLE	ACT_DECKS	ACT_SEATS
2	Boeing 767	Wide	Single	350
3	Boeing 737	Narrow	Single	200
4	Boeing 757	Narrow	Single	240

Changing the order of the conditions in the SELECT statement would also have altered the results. The better option is the parentheses, however. Parentheses make it clear from the outset which conditions are evaluated together.

```
SELECT  *
FROM    aircraft_types
WHERE   act_body_style != 'Wide'
OR      act_seats > 200
AND     act_decks = 'Single';

ACT_ID ACT_NAME     ACT_BODY_STYLE ACT_DECKS  ACT_SEATS
------ ------------ -------------- ---------- ---------
     2 Boeing 767   Wide           Single           350
     3 Boeing 737   Narrow         Single           200
     4 Boeing 757   Narrow         Single           240
```

The NOT logical operator simply reverses a given operator. The statement below has the condition 'WHERE NOT act_decks = 'Single'. This could just as easily be written 'WHERE act_decks != 'Single'. However, NOT is the only practical way to reverse the BETWEEN, IN, IS NULL, or LIKE operators.

```
SELECT  *
FROM    aircraft_types
WHERE   NOT act_decks = 'Single';

ACT_ID ACT_NAME     ACT_BODY_STYLE ACT_DECKS  ACT_SEATS
------ ------------ -------------- ---------- ---------
     1 Boeing 747   Wide           Double           416
```

Precedence in WHERE clauses

When evaluating a WHERE clause, the order in which Oracle executes each of the conditions and operations is of critical importance in what the final result will be. The rules of precedence according to the Oracle SQL Reference manual are:

1. Arithmetic Operators (+, - , *, /)
2. Concatenation Operator (| |)
3. Comparison conditions (=, !=, <, >, <=, >=)
4. IS [NOT] NULL, LIKE, [NOT] BETWEEN, [NOT] IN, EXISTS, IS OF type
5. NOT logical condition
6. AND logical condition
7. OR logical condition

You can override the default order of precedence by making use of parenthesis. When you have a particularly complex clause, adding parenthesis is often advisable even if not strictly required in order to make the order of precedence more evident.

Sort the rows that are retrieved by a query

The ORDER BY clause of a SQL query allows you to order the rows returned by the operation. When a SQL statement does not contain an ORDER BY clause, the order of the rows being returned is indeterminate. When the ORDER BY clause is used, it must be the last clause of the SQL statement.

It's possible to sort by a single column or by multiple columns (or expressions). When sorting by multiple columns, the precedence of the sort order will be determined by the position of the expression in the ORDER BY clause. The leftmost expression will provide the initial sort order and each expression to the right will be evaluated in turn. By default, data is sorted in ascending order (1-2-3-4 / a-b-c-d). One item of note is the fact that upper and lower case characters don't sort together. When Oracle sorts by character values, it is actually using the ASCII values for the logic. Because of this, a lower case 'a' will sort *higher* than an upper case 'Z'. In addition, numeric data in a character field does not sort as you would expect. For example, if you were to sort table rows with values containing '1', '2', and '100' in ascending order, the result would be 1-100-2. To sort number data in a character field in numeric order, you would have to use the TO_NUMBER function against the column in the ORDER BY clause to convert the data for sort purposes. Of course if the column contains non-numerics, using TO_NUMBER is liable to generate an error.

By default NULLS are sorted last when a sort is in ascending order and first when descending. Effectively when being sorted, NULLs are treated as an infinitely high value. The default behavior can be reversed by adding NULLS LAST when sorting in descending order or NULLS FIRST when sorting in ascending order.

It is not possible to use LONG or LOB columns in an ORDER BY clause.

When specifying the expressions to sort by, you can use either the expression itself, the alias for the expression, or the numeric value of its position in the SELECT list. Using the position rather than the expression can be useful of the expression being sorted on is complex. It is also useful when sorting compound queries using the set operators (UNION, INTERSECT, MINUS) where the column names may not match. Set operators will be discussed in a later section.

```
SELECT *
FROM    airports
ORDER BY apt_name;

APT_ID APT_NAME                              APT_ABBR
------ ----------------------------- --------
     2 Atlanta, GA                           ATL
     5 Dallas/Fort Worth                     DFW
     4 Jacksonville, FL                      JAX
     3 Miami, FL                             MIA
     1 Orlando, FL                           MCO
```

```
SELECT  *
FROM    airports
ORDER BY 2;

APT_ID APT_NAME                         APT_ABBR
------ ------------------------------ --------
     2 Atlanta, GA                       ATL
     5 Dallas/Fort Worth                 DFW
     4 Jacksonville, FL                  JAX
     3 Miami, FL                         MIA
     1 Orlando, FL                       MCO
```

To reverse the sort order of columns, you can use the descending operator, DESC.

```
SELECT  *
FROM    airports
ORDER BY 2 DESC;

APT_ID APT_NAME                 APT_ABBR
------ ---------------------- --------
     1 Orlando, FL               MCO
     3 Miami, FL                 MIA
     4 Jacksonville, FL          JAX
     5 Dallas/Fort Worth         DFW
     2 Atlanta, GA               ATL
```

The default sort order on columns is always ascending. If a column is sorted on more than one column, and you want to change multiple columns to sort in descending order, each would need its own DESC keyword. The following query sorts by three columns. First it sorts all the rows by the EMP_JOB field in ascending order. For all employees in the same job, it sorts rows by the AIRCRAFT_TYPE in descending order. For all rows with the same job and aircraft type, it sorts in ascending order by last name.

```
SELECT emp_job,
        (SELECT act_name
         FROM   aircraft_types act
                NATURAL JOIN aircraft_fleet afl
          WHERE afl.afl_id = e1.afl_id) AS aircraft_type,
        emp_last,
        (SELECT emp_last
         FROM employees e2
         WHERE e2.emp_id = e1.emp_supervisor) AS MANAGER
FROM    employees e1
ORDER BY emp_job, aircraft_type DESC, emp_last;
```

EMP_JOB	AIRCRAFT_TYPE	EMP_LAST	MANAGER
CEO		Boss	
CFO		Smith	Boss
Mgr		Storm	Alien
Pilot	Boeing 767	Gun	Storm
Pilot	Boeing 767	Jones	Storm
Pilot	Boeing 767	Kia	Storm
Pilot	Boeing 757	Thomas	Storm
Pilot	Boeing 747	Aptop	Storm
Pilot	Boeing 747	Picard	Storm
Pilot	Boeing 747	Skytalker	Storm
Pilot	Boeing 737	McCoy	Storm
SVP		Jameson	Boss
SVP		Stoner	Boss
SrDir		Alien	Jeckson
SrDir		Stoneflint	Abong
VP		Abong	Jameson
VP		Jeckson	Stoner

Use ampersand substitution to restrict and sort output at runtime

The ampersand symbol '&' is used in the SQL*Plus and SQL Developer tools to add a substitution variable to a SQL statement. Substitution variables allow you to build scripts that are not 100% fixed to run the same way every time they are executed. By replacing portions of one or more parts of a SQL statement with ampersands, you can cause the tool to replace parts of the SQL with data that will be supplied at run-time. Substitution variables can be used to replace the following:

- Column Expressions
- Table names
- WHERE conditions
- ORDER BY clauses
- Complete SELECT statements

When the following SQL statement is executed, a dialog box will open up requesting a value for the substitution variable AIRCRAFT_NAME. Note that the substitution variable is enclosed in quotes. The tool will take the information you supply, swap it for the substitution variable verbatim, and then run the SQL. Since the below statement is a character field, it must be enclosed in quotes. If the substitution variable were not enclosed in quotes, you would have to quote the value entered in the dialog or the statement would result in an error.

```
SELECT act_name, act_body_style, act_decks
FROM   aircraft_types
WHERE  act_name = '&AIRCRAFT_NAME';
```

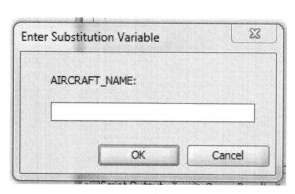

Once the dialog box has been populated and the OK button clicked, the query will continue and produce results with the new value. By default, the tool will also provide information about the replacement that was just performed.

```
old:SELECT act_name, act_body_style, act_decks
FROM   aircraft_types
WHERE  act_name = '&AIRCRAFT_NAME'
new:SELECT act_name, act_body_style, act_decks
FROM   aircraft_types
WHERE  act_name = 'Boeing 767'
```

```
ACT_NAME       ACT_BODY_STYLE ACT_DECKS
------------   -------------- ----------
Boeing 767     Wide           Single
```

The following example has substitution variables set up for a column, a WHERE clause condition, and the ORDER BY clause. The user can specify each of these values at run time:

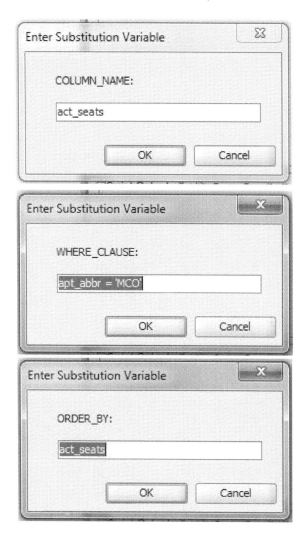

```
SELECT apt_name, apt_abbr, act_name, &COLUMN_NAME
FROM   aircraft_fleet_v
WHERE  &WHERE_CLAUSE
ORDER BY &ORDER_BY

old:SELECT apt_name, apt_abbr, act_name, &COLUMN_NAME
FROM   aircraft_fleet_v
WHERE  &WHERE_CLAUSE
ORDER BY &ORDER_BY
new:SELECT apt_name, apt_abbr, act_name, act_seats
FROM   aircraft_fleet_v
WHERE  apt_abbr = 'MCO'
ORDER BY act_seats
```

```
APT_NAME                 APT_ABBR ACT_NAME       ACT_SEATS
-------------------      -------- ------------   ---------
Orlando, FL              MCO      Boeing 767           350
Orlando, FL              MCO      Boeing 767           350
```

The text returned by SQL*Plus and SQL Developer that shows the old and new versions of a SQL statement using substitution variables is part of the VERIFY function. You can turn this capability off by issuing the command SET VERIFY OFF. Likewise, if you have turned it off but wish to re-enable it, you can issue the SET VERIFY ON command.

All of the examples so far have used one variant of the substitution variable. Substitution variables can be specified with either a single ampersand or with a pair of ampersands. The behavior difference is that when a substitution variable is specified with two ampersands, it is possible to re-use the variable in another portion of the statement without having to prompt the user again. The value is persistent, in fact, not just for the remainder of the statement but for the Oracle session as well. If the script were to be run a second time, the user would not be prompted for the variable.

```
SELECT apt_name, apt_abbr, act_name, &&COLUMN_NAME
FROM   aircraft_fleet_v
ORDER BY &COLUMN_NAME

ORDER BY act_seats
APT_NAME                 APT_ABBR ACT_NAME       ACT_SEATS
-------------------      -------- ------------   ---------
Atlanta, GA              ATL      Boeing 737           200
Atlanta, GA              ATL      Boeing 757           240
Orlando, FL              MCO      Boeing 767           350
Dallas/Fort Worth        DFW      Boeing 767           350
Orlando, FL              MCO      Boeing 767           350
Dallas/Fort Worth        DFW      Boeing 747           416
Miami, FL                MIA      Boeing 747           416
Miami, FL                MIA      Boeing 747           416
```

DEFINE and UNDEFINE

The DEFINE command is used to set a substitution variable to a given value. If the DEFINE command is used to set the value of a variable prior to running a SQL statement that makes use of it, the user won't be prompted for the value. The double-ampersand works by accepting the variable supplied by the user, and then performing an implicit DEFINE so that the value won't be requested again in the current session. The UNDEFINE command is used to clear a substitution variable value (so that the next SQL statement using that variable will prompt the user for a value).

```
DEFINE variable_name
UNDEFINE variable_name
```

Using Single-Row Functions to Customize Output

Functions are an extremely important part of Oracle's capabilities. Functions will sometimes accept one or more arguments, but they will always return a value when called. When a single row functions is included in a SQL query, it will generate one result for each table row returned. By contrast, a multiple-row function will return one result for a given set of rows. Single row functions can be used in the following locations:

- SELECT lists
- WHERE clauses
- START WITH clauses
- CONNECT BY clauses
- HAVING clauses

Describe various types of functions available in SQL

SQL functions are built into the Oracle Database and can be used in various SQL statements. SQL functions should not be confused with user-defined functions written in PL/SQL. There are too many SQL functions available in Oracle to discuss all of them in this guide. I'll define some of the more common functions that might appear on the test. Before attempting the test, you should investigate the SQL Functions in the Oracle SQL Language Reference book. You are almost certain to see some on the test that are not in this guide and you will need some familiarity with what they do.

There are five distinct types of single row functions available in Oracle.
- **Numeric** – Accept numeric input and return numeric results.
- **Character** – Accept character input and return character or numeric results.
- **Datetime** – Perform work on date data types and return date or numeric results.
- **Conversion** – Convert from one data type to another.
- **General** – Perform functions that don't fit the above four descriptions.

44

Numeric Functions

ABS
Syntax: ABS(*n*)
Purpose: ABS returns the absolute value of *n*.

```
SELECT ABS(-5) "Abs_Ex"
FROM dual;

Abs_Ex
----------
5
```

CEIL
Syntax: CEIL(*n*)
Purpose: CEIL returns the smallest integer that is greater than or equal to *n*.

```
SELECT CEIL(2343.2) "Ceil_Ex"
FROM dual;

Ceil_Ex
-----------
2344
```

FLOOR
Syntax: FLOOR(*n*)
Purpose: FLOOR returns the largest integer equal to or less than *n*.

```
SELECT FLOOR(21.2) "Floor_Ex"
FROM dual;

Floor_Ex
----------
21
```

ROUND(number)
Syntax: ROUND(*n, integer*)
Purpose: ROUND returns *n* rounded to *integer* places to the right of the decimal point. If *integer* is not supplied, then *n* is rounded to zero places. If the *integer* value is negative, then *n* is rounded off to the left of the decimal point.

```
SELECT ROUND(127.623, 1)  "Round_Ex1",
```

```
      ROUND(127.623)      "Round_Ex2",
      ROUND(127.623, -1) "Round_Ex3"
FROM dual;

Round_Ex1   Round_Ex2   Round_Ex3
----------  ----------  ----------
127.6       127         120
```

Character Functions

INITCAP
Syntax: INITCAP(*char*)
Purpose: INITCAP returns *char*, with the first letter of each word in uppercase, and all other letters in lowercase. The delimiter used to determine words are white space or non alphanumeric characters.

```
SELECT INITCAP('john jones') "Initcap_Ex"
FROM dual;

Initcap_Ex
---------
John Jones
```

LOWER
Syntax: LOWER (*char*)
Purpose: LOWER returns *char*, with all letters lowercase.

```
SELECT LOWER('John Jones') "Lower_Ex"
FROM DUAL;

Lower_EX
----------------
john jones
```

LPAD
Syntax: LPAD(*expr1, n, expr2*)
Purpose: LPAD returns *expr1*, left-padded to length *n* characters with the sequence of characters in *expr2*. If *expr2* is not specified, then the default value is a single space.

```
SELECT LPAD('Page 1', 14, '.') "Lpad_Ex"
FROM DUAL;

Lpad_Ex
--------------
........Page 1
```

LTRIM

Syntax: TRIM(*char, set*)

Purpose: LTRIM removes from the left end of *char* all of the characters contained in *set*. If *set* is not specified, it defaults to a single space.

```
SELECT LTRIM('\----/DATA\----/', '/\-') "Ltrim_Ex"
FROM DUAL;

Ltrim_Ex
----------
DATA\----/
```

LENGTH

Syntax: LENGTH(*char*)

Purpose: The LENGTH functions return the length of *char*. LENGTH calculates length using characters as defined by the input character set.

```
SELECT LENGTH('1Z0-047') "Length_Ex"
FROM DUAL;

Length_Ex
----------
7
```

Datetime Functions

ADD_MONTHS

Syntax: ADD_MONTHS(*date, integer*)

Purpose: ADD_MONTHS returns the supplied *date* plus *integer* months.

```
SELECT TO_CHAR(ADD_MONTHS('10-MAR-11', 1), 'DD-MON-YY')
"Add_months_Ex"
FROM dual;

Add_months_Ex
-------------
10-APR-11
```

LAST_DAY
Syntax: LAST_DAY(*date*)
Purpose: Returns the last day of the month that contains *date*.

```
SELECT LAST_DAY('12-MAR-11') "Last_day_Ex"
FROM dual;

Last_day_Ex
-----------
30-MAY-09
```

MONTHS_BETWEEN
Syntax: MONTHS_BETWEEN(*date1, date2*)
Purpose: MONTHS_BETWEEN returns number of months between *date1* and *date2*. If *date1* is later than *date2*, then the result is positive. If *date1* is earlier than *date2*, then the result is negative. If *date1* and *date2* are either the same days of the month or both last days of months, then the result is an integer.

```
SELECT MONTHS_BETWEEN('02-JAN-12', '04-JUN-12')
"Months_Between_Ex"
FROM DUAL;

Months_Between_Ex
-----------------
-5.0645161290322580645161290322580645161613
```

NEXT_DAY
Syntax: NEXT_DAY(*date, char*)
Purpose: NEXT_DAY returns the date of the first weekday named by *char* that is later than *date*. The return type is always DATE, regardless of the data type of date.

```
SELECT NEXT_DAY('03-MAR-12','FRIDAY') "Next_day_Ex"
FROM dual;

Next_day_Ex
--------------
09-MAR-12
```

Conversion Functions

TO_NUMBER
Syntax: TO_NUMBER(expr, fmt, 'nlsparam')
Purpose: TO_NUMBER converts expr to a value of NUMBER data type. The expr can be a BINARY_DOUBLE value or a value of character data type containing a number in the format specified by the optional format model fmt.The optional 'nlsparam' argument specifies the language in which the number format is returned.

```
SELECT  TO_NUMBER('$4,355.80',  'FML999G990D00') "To_Num_Ex"
FROM    dual;

To_Num_Ex
---------
4355.8
```

TO_CHAR
Syntax: TO_CHAR(datetime, fmt, 'nlsparam')
Purpose: Converts a datetime to a value of VARCHAR2 data type in the format specified by the date format fmt. The optional 'nlsparam' argument specifies the language in which month and day names and abbreviations are returned.

```
SELECT TO_CHAR(SYSDATE, 'Day, Month DD, YYYY') AS
"To_Char_Ex"
FROM    dual;

To_Char_Ex
----------------------------
Saturday , April      07, 2012
```

TO_DATE
Syntax: TO_DATE(char, fmt, 'nlsparam')
Purpose: TO_DATE converts char of a character data type to a value of DATE data type. The fmt is a datetime model format specifying the format of char. The 'nlsparam' argument specifies the language of the text string that is being converted to a date.

```
SELECT TO_DATE('Saturday , April     07, 2012 ',
               'Day, Month DD, YYYY') AS "To_Date_Ex"
FROM    dual;

To_Date_Ex
----------
07-APR-12
```

General Functions

NVL
Syntax: NVL(expr1, expr2)
Purpose: NVL will replace NULL with a string. If expr1 is NULL, then NVL returns expr2. If expr1 is not NULL, then NVL returns expr1.

```
SELECT NVL('', 'Value is NULL') "Nvl_Ex1",
       NVL(dummy, 'Value is NULL') "Nvl_Ex2"
FROM    dual;

Nvl_Ex1        Nvl_Ex2
-------------- --------------
Value is NULL X
```

NULLIF
Syntax: NULLIF(expr1, expr2)
Purpose: If expr1 and expr2 are equal, then NULLIF returns null. If they are not equal, then is returns expr1. You cannot specify the literal NULL for expr1.

```
SELECT NULLIF(dummy, 'X') "Nullif_Ex2"
FROM    dual;

Nullif_Ex2
----------
```

Use character, number, and date functions in SELECT statements

Character Functions

The character functions of Oracle modify or provide information regarding character datatypes in Oracle. Character SQL functions can be used in the SELECT clause in order to modify the data returned by a statement, such as the following that transforms airport names to upper-case:

```
SELECT UPPER(apt_name) APT_NAME, apt_abbr
FROM   airports

APT_NAME                            APT_ABBR
-----------------------------       --------
ORLANDO, FL                         MCO
ATLANTA, GA                         ATL
MIAMI, FL                           MIA
JACKSONVILLE, FL                    JAX
DALLAS/FORT WORTH                   DFW
```

The INITCAP function works similarly to the UPPER function except that it capitalizes only the initial letter of each word:

```
SELECT INITCAP(apt_name) APT_NAME, apt_abbr
FROM   airports

APT_NAME                  APT_ABBR
--------------------      --------
Orlando, Fl               MCO
Atlanta, Ga               ATL
Miami, Fl                 MIA
Jacksonville, Fl          JAX
Dallas/Fort Worth         DFW
```

You can also use SQL functions in the WHERE clause to create custom conditions that will locate specific rows. In the example below, the airport name is upper cased, and then the third character pulled out via the SUBSTR function to return all airports with an 'L' or 'l' as the third letter.

```
SELECT apt_name, apt_abbr
FROM   airports
WHERE  SUBSTR(UPPER(apt_name), 3, 1) = 'L'

APT_NAME                              APT_ABBR
----------------------------------    --------
Orlando, FL                           MCO
Atlanta, GA                           ATL
Dallas/Fort Worth                     DFW
```

Numeric Functions

Just as character functions alter or provide information about character data, numeric functions perform operations against numeric data. Unlike character and date functions, numeric functions always accept AND return a numeric value. In the following example, the annual salary of employees is divided by the number of hours in a work year, and the result rounded to two decimal places with the ROUND function:

```
SELECT emp_first, emp_last, ROUND(salary / 2080, 2) AS
HOURLY_SAL
FROM    employees
WHERE   emp_job = 'Pilot';

EMP_FIRST   EMP_LAST    HOURLY_SAL
----------  ----------  ----------
John        Jones            46.88
Top         Gun              43.99
Phil        McCoy            50.48
James       Thomas           47.36
John        Picard            23.8
Luke        Skytalker        43.27
Dell        Aptop            42.07
Noh         Kia              44.35
```

The TRUNC function performs a function similar ROUND. However, where the ROUND function will perform a rounding operation on decimal values to the right of the defined precision, TRUNC simply removes all numbers to the right of the defined precision. In the example below, Jones, Thomas, Picard, Skytalker, and Aptop are all shown a penny lower because the tenths of a penny were truncated rather then rounded.

```
SELECT emp_first, emp_last, TRUNC(salary / 2080, 2) AS
HOURLY_SAL
FROM    employees
WHERE   emp_job = 'Pilot';
```

```
EMP_FIRST   EMP_LAST    HOURLY_SAL
----------  ----------  ----------
John        Jones            46.87
Top         Gun              43.99
Phil        McCoy            50.48
James       Thomas           47.35
John        Picard           23.79
Luke        Skytalker        43.26
Dell        Aptop            42.06
Noh         Kia              44.35
```

Date Functions

Oracle stores date data in an internal format that contains century, year, month, day, hours, minutes, and seconds. Oracle can store dates between January 1, 4712 B.C. and December 31, 9999 A.D. That means that in a little less than 8000 years, someone is going to predict the world will end on Dec 31, 9999 because Larry Ellison said it would.

Date SQL functions are used to transform information in DATE data types. In the below example, the MONTHS_BETWEEN function is used to determine the number of months it has been since each of the pilots was hired. Note that while two DATE types are passed to the function, a NUMBER type is returned. The value returned by SQL functions is not always the same as the value passed to it.

```
SELECT emp_first, emp_last, MONTHS_BETWEEN(SYSDATE,
start_date) AS months_since_hire
FROM    employees
WHERE   emp_job = 'Pilot';
```

```
EMP_FIRST       EMP_LAST        MONTHS_SINCE_HIRE
------------    --------------  -----------------
John            Jones           203.577734841696535244922341169
Top             Gun             185.480960648148148148148148148
Phil            McCoy           189.609992906212664277718040621
James           Thomas          154.513218712664277718040621266
John            Picard          124.545476777180406212664277718
Luke            Skytalker       114.577734841696535244922341169
Dell            Aptop           103.190638067502986857825567506
Noh             Kia             92.6745090352449223416965352444
```

The MONTH_SINCE_HIRE value is really awkward in the above example. Because the result of the MONTHS_BETWEEN function is a NUMBER type, we can apply the numeric function TRUNC to the result to clean it up:

```
SELECT emp_first, emp_last, TRUNC(MONTHS_BETWEEN(SYSDATE,
start_date)) AS months_since_hire
FROM    employees
WHERE   emp_job = 'Pilot';
```

EMP_FIRST	EMP_LAST	MONTHS_SINCE_HIRE
John	Jones	203
Top	Gun	185
Phil	McCoy	189
James	Thomas	154
John	Picard	124
Luke	Skytalker	114
Dell	Aptop	103
Noh	Kia	92

Performing Date Calculations

Not only is the Oracle date format numeric, but it is stored in such a way that a single day equals one. The means that if you take a given date value and add the number three to it, the resulting value is exactly three days later than the original date value. Likewise you can subtract three from a given date and the result date will be exactly three days prior to the original. The following two examples demonstrate adding and subtracting the number three from the current date.

```
SELECT TO_CHAR(SYSDATE, 'DD-MON HH24:MI:SS') AS SYS_DATE,
       TO_CHAR(SYSDATE + 3, 'DD-MON HH24:MI:SS') AS SYS_DATE
FROM   dual;
```

SYS_DATE	SYS_DATE
07-APR 21:28:10	10-APR 21:28:10

```
SELECT TO_CHAR(SYSDATE, 'DD-MON HH24:MI:SS') AS SYS_DATE,
       TO_CHAR(SYSDATE - 3, 'DD-MON HH24:MI:SS') AS SYS_DATE
FROM   dual;
```

SYS_DATE	SYS_DATE
07-APR 21:28:42	04-APR 21:28:42

Just as the number one represents a single day, fractions of 1 represent a fraction of a day. To add or subtract hours from a date, you can use increments of 1/24 (one hour). To add or subtract minutes from a date, you can use increments of 1/1440 (there are 1440 minutes in a day). The following two examples demonstrate this. The first subtracts seven hours from the current date, and the second subtracts 22 minutes.

```
SELECT TO_CHAR(SYSDATE, 'DD-MON HH24:MI:SS') AS SYS_DATE,
       TO_CHAR(SYSDATE - 7/24, 'DD-MON HH24:MI:SS')
            AS SYS_DATE_TR
FROM   dual;

SYS_DATE                 SYS_DATE_TR
------------------------ ------------------------
07-APR 21:29:16          07-APR 14:29:16


SELECT TO_CHAR(SYSDATE, 'DD-MON HH24:MI:SS') AS SYS_DATE,
       TO_CHAR(SYSDATE - 22/1440, 'DD-MON HH24:MI:SS')
            AS SYS_DATE_TR
FROM   dual;

SYS_DATE                 SYS_DATE_TR
------------------------ ------------------------
07-APR 21:33:52          07-APR 21:11:52
```

One interesting function not normally associated with dates is TRUNC. Because dates are numeric, the TRUNC function can be used to modify the date value. When applied against a date with no format specified, it removes the decimal portion (the part of a day past midnight). When a format is supplied, you can truncate to the start of the most recent hour, month or year (among other possibilities). It's also possible to use the ROUND function with dates.

```
SELECT TO_CHAR(SYSDATE, 'DD-MON HH24:MI:SS') AS SYS_DATE,
       TO_CHAR(TRUNC(SYSDATE), 'DD-MON HH24:MI:SS')
            AS TRUNC_DAY
FROM   dual;

SYS_DATE                 TRUNC_DAY
------------------------ ------------------------
07-APR 21:42:54          07-APR 00:00:00
```

```
SELECT  TO_CHAR(SYSDATE, 'DD-MON HH24:MI:SS') AS SYS_DATE,
        TO_CHAR(TRUNC(SYSDATE, 'HH'), 'DD-MON HH24:MI:SS')
               AS TRUNC_HOUR
FROM    dual;

SYS_DATE                    TRUNC_HOUR
------------------------    ------------------------
07-APR 21:42:54             07-APR 21:00:00


SELECT  TO_CHAR(SYSDATE, 'DD-MON HH24:MI:SS') AS SYS_DATE,
        TO_CHAR(TRUNC(SYSDATE, 'MM'), 'DD-MON HH24:MI:SS')
               AS TRUNC_MONTH
FROM    dual;

SYS_DATE                    TRUNC_MONTH
------------------------    ------------------------
07-APR 21:43:26             01-APR 00:00:00


SELECT  TO_CHAR(SYSDATE, 'DD-MON HH24:MI:SS') AS SYS_DATE,
        TO_CHAR(TRUNC(SYSDATE, 'YYYY'), 'DD-MON HH24:MI:SS')
               AS TRUNC_YEAR
FROM    dual;

SYS_DATE                    TRUNC_YEAR
------------------------    ------------------------
07-APR 21:43:49             01-JAN 00:00:00
```

RR date Format

This date format was a product of the Y2K hysteria in the late 90s. For years two-digits had been used as shorthand to represent a four-digit year and suddenly everyone realized that the millennium was about to end and reset the numbering scheme. The RR date format was designed to allow existing interfaces with two-digit years to be used and have the database logically determine what millennium and century the user intended. The RR logic makes use of the current two-digit year and compares it to the supplied two-digit year to determine what was meant.

- If current year is 0-49 and supplied year is 0-49, use current century.
- If current year is 50-99 and supplied year is 50-99, use current century.
- If current year is 0-49 and supplied year is 50-99, use prior century.
- If current year is 50-99 and supplied year is 0-49, use next century.

Keep in mind that this logic isn't always correct. For example, it would make the wrong choice if you were entering a birth date into Oracle for someone who was born in 1932. The RR logic would store this value as 2032. For numbers that can span decades, you should really make use of a four-digit year so that the is no ambiguity whatsoever in the meaning.

Using Conversion Functions and Conditional Expressions

From what's been presented so far, it's clear that the separation between data types isn't always as complete as it would appear at first glance. For example, dates are stored as a number and can have arithmetic performed on them but are always displayed as character data. For this reason, it's an extremely common occurrence for the Oracle server to receive data in one data type when it expects a different one. When that happens, there must be a conversion operation.

Describe various types of conversion functions that are available in SQL

Implicit Conversion

Any time a SQL function is called with an argument of a data type other than the one expected, Oracle will make an attempt to convert the argument to the expected type. If the conversion is successful, then Oracle will perform the SQL function with no outward indication that the conversion took place. If the conversion is unsuccessful, the operation will fail, and an error will be generated.

This automatic process is called implicit conversion. Oracle is so good at implicit conversion that the only time you realize that a conversion operation is taking place is when something prevents it from doing so and you get an error.

The implicit conversion of number to character and date to character is seamless and the conversion itself will never generate errors. Any number value can also be a character value, and a date value will always be implicitly converted to a character format matching the current NLS_DATE_FORMAT parameter (or the default of 'DD-MON-YY' if that parameter isn't set).

Implicit conversion of character to number only works when the character is a valid number. Implicitly converting '2354' to number will succeed whereas implicitly converting '14a', '2,423', or '$12.52' will fail because non-numeric elements are present in the character string. Likewise converting a character to a date implicitly will succeed only if the character data matches the current NLS_DATE_FORMAT parameter. If there is anything that prevents an implicit conversion from taking place, you must explicitly convert the data.

Explicit Conversion

Despite how good Oracle is at implicit conversion, it's not really good practice to rely on it. When implicit conversion fails, it generates errors and stops whatever process was being performed. The recommended practice is that you use the available functions where there is a need to convert data from one data type into the required data type. This is known as explicit conversion. The three most common conversion functions are:

- **TO_CHAR** – Converts a number or date value into a character data type.
- **TO_NUMBER** – Converts a character string into a number data type.
- **TO_DATE** – Converts a character or number data type into a date data type.

There are other conversion functions – notably some involving LOB or Large Object data types. However, you are very unlikely to see these on the exam. To learn more about them, you should make use of the Oracle SQL Reference Manual.

Use the TO_CHAR, TO_NUMBER, and TO_DATE conversion functions

Using the TO_CHAR function

The TO_CHAR function has three variants depending on the input data type: TO_CHAR (character), TO_CHAR(datetime), and TO_CHAR(number). One of the three is used to convert multibyte characters or CLOB data to a VARCHAR2 data type and is unlikely to be represented on the test. This guide will deal with the second two variants.

TO_CHAR
Syntax: TO_CHAR(datetime, 'fmt', 'nlsparam')
Purpose: TO_CHAR (datetime) converts a datetime or interval value of DATE, TIMESTAMP, TIMESTAMP WITH TIME ZONE, TIMESTAMP WITH LOCAL TIME ZONE, INTERVAL DAY TO SECOND, or INTERVAL YEAR TO MONTH data type to a value of VARCHAR2 data type in the format specified by the date format fmt.

The following example demonstrates converting (and splitting) the system date into separate date and time values.

```
SELECT  TO_CHAR(SYSDATE, 'YYYY, MON DD') AS TC_DATE,
        TO_CHAR(SYSDATE, 'HH:MI AM') AS TC_TIME
FROM    dual;

TC_DATE               TC_TIME
--------------------  --------
2012, APR 07          11:23 PM
```

TO_CHAR
Syntax: TO_CHAR(n, 'fmt', 'nlsparam')
Purpose: TO_CHAR (number) converts n to a value of VARCHAR2 data type, using the optional number format fmt. If you omit fmt, then n is converted to a VARCHAR2 value exactly long enough to hold its significant digits. When the nlsparam value is specified, it determines the decimal character, group separator, local currency symbol, and the international currency symbol of the returned value.

```
SELECT TO_CHAR('4235.34','FML9,999.99') "To_char_Ex"
FROM dual;

To_char_Ex
-------------------
$4,235.34
```

Using the TO_NUMBER function

The TO_NUMBER function of Oracle is generally used when you have
numeric data that is currently in a character data type and you need to
perform arithmetic on it, pass it to a function expecting a numeric
argument, or store it in a NUMBER field of a table. Oracle's implicit
conversion works extremely well when character data is already
formatted as a bare number. The most common use of TO_NUMBER is
when the character string contains non-numeric aspects. This might be
dollar signs, commas, or other formatting elements that will prevent
Oracle from being able to determine the specific numeric value to convert
the string to.

TO_NUMBER
Syntax: TO_NUMBER(expr, fmt, 'nlsparam')
Purpose: Converts *expr* to a value of NUMBER data type. The *expr* can be
a BINARY_DOUBLE value or a character data type containing a number in
the format specified by the optional format model *fmt*. The optional
'nlsparam' argument specifies the language of the char input.

```
SELECT TO_NUMBER('$4235.34','FML9,999.99') "To_number_Ex"
FROM dual;

To_number_Ex
------------
4235.34
```

```
SELECT TO_NUMBER('3.4E+05', '9.9EEEE')
FROM    dual;

TO_NUMBER('3.4E+05','9.9EEEE')
-----------------------------
                        340000
```

Using the TO_DATE Function

As with the TO_NUMBER function, you are required to use the TO_DATE conversion function when a character value is in a date format that Oracle does not recognize implicitly. The default date format that Oracle uses is DD-MON-YY. This default can be altered by setting the parameter NLS_DATE_FORMAT for either the session or the database. The TO_DATE function, however, can be used to convert text to a date from any format that can be expressed with a date format string. The date format strings in Oracle are flexible enough that this evaluates to effectively any date format.

TO_DATE
Syntax: TO_DATE(char, fmt, 'nlsparam')
Purpose: Converts character data to a value of DATE data type. fmt is a datetime model format matching the char input. If fmt is omitted, char must be in the default date format. The optional 'nlsparam' argument specifies the language of the char input.

```
SELECT TO_DATE('February 23, 2012, 2:23 P.M.', 'Month dd,
YYYY, HH:MI A.M.') AS "To_date_Ex"
FROM DUAL;

To_date_Ex
----------
23-FEB-12
```

Most of the conversion formats from character to date are alphanumeric. The exception is a Julian date. When using TO_DATE to convert a Julian date, the char value must evaluate to an integer value. The integer can be enclosed in single quotes or not.

```
SELECT TO_DATE(2456029, 'J') AS "To_date_Ex"
FROM dual;

To_date_Ex
----------
11-APR-12
```

The fx format modifier alters the behavior of Oracle's format checking when it is included as part of the format model. FX stands for 'format exact' and forces the character data being checked to match <u>exactly</u> with the supplied format model. Using the previous example, an extra space is added before '2012'. The format model supplied in the previous example is still able to recognize the date.

```
SELECT TO_DATE('February 23,  2012, 2:23 P.M.', 'Month dd,
YYYY, HH:MI A.M.') AS "To_date_Ex"
FROM DUAL;

To_date_Ex
----------
23-FEB-12
```

However, when the 'fx' modifier is placed in front of the format model and the statement executed again, the conversion fails because the format model expects only a single space between the comma and year.

```
SELECT TO_DATE('February 23,  2012, 2:23 P.M.', 'fxMonth dd,
YYYY, HH:MI A.M.') AS "To_date_Ex"
FROM DUAL;

SQL Error: ORA-01841: (full) year must be between -4713 and
+9999, and not be 0
01841. 00000 -  "(full) year must be between -4713 and +9999,
and not be 0"
*Cause:    Illegal year entered
*Action:   Input year in the specified range
```

Apply conditional expressions in a SELECT statement

Conditional functions provide SQL statements with the ability to perform IF-THEN-ELSE decisions. This is a very useful capability as it gives SQL a small portion of the procedural capabilities that otherwise requires PL/SQL. The two conditional expressions that can be performed within SQL in Oracle are CASE and DECODE. The CASE function is part of the capabilities defined within the ANSI SQL specification. The DECODE statement is an Oracle-specific function.

The syntax for a CASE statement is:

```
CASE expr
    WHEN comp_1 THEN return_1;
    [WHEN comp_2 THEN return_2, …]
    ELSE return_else
END CASE;
```

In processing a CASE statement, Oracle will evaluate the WHEN conditions from top-down. As soon as any of the conditions evaluates to TRUE, the evaluation process stops and the value listed in the current WHEN condition is returned by the CASE statement. If none of the WHEN conditions evaluates to TRUE, the value in the ELSE condition is returned by the CASE statement. If a CASE statement doesn't match any of the supplied WHEN conditions and no ELSE condition is provided, Oracle will generate an error. The following CASE example provides a return value that depends on the employee's job title.

```
SELECT emp_first || ' ' || emp_last,
       CASE emp_job
           WHEN 'CEO' THEN 'This is the big Kahuna'
           WHEN 'CFO' THEN 'The dude holding the piggy bank'
           WHEN 'SVP' THEN 'Senior right-hand guy'
           WHEN 'VP' THEN 'Right-hand guy'
           WHEN 'SrDir' THEN 'Middle Management'
           WHEN 'Mgr' THEN 'Lower Management'
           ELSE 'Just another peon'
       END CASE
FROM    employees
ORDER BY emp_id;

EMP_FIRST||''||EMP_LAST CASE
----------------------- -------------------------------
Big Boss                This is the big Kahuna
Adam Smith              The dude holding the piggy bank
Rick Jameson            Senior right-hand guy
Rob Stoner              Senior right-hand guy
Bill Abong              Right-hand guy
Janet Jeckson           Right-hand guy
Fred Stoneflint         Middle Management
Alf Alien               Middle Management
Norm Storm              Lower Management
John Jones              Just another peon
Top Gun                 Just another peon
Phil McCoy              Just another peon
James Thomas            Just another peon
John Picard        -    Just another peon
Luke Skytalker          Just another peon
Dell Aptop              Just another peon
Noh Kia                 Just another peon
```

The DECODE statement predates Oracle's implementation of the CASE capability. It provides a similar capability to CASE, but is not quite as flexible. It is designed to evaluate equality only, whereas CASE can use multiple conditional operators (>, <, !=, etc.) In addition, when a DECODE statement is evaluating multiple conditions, it becomes difficult to read. The syntax for DECODE is:

```
DECODE(expr, search, result [,search2, result2…], default)
```

A DECODE function compares the value of expr to each search value one by one. If expr is equal to a search value, then processing stops and the function returns the corresponding result. If no match is found, the default is returned. If there is no default, then the DECODE returns null. All of those are identical to the behavior of a CASE except the last.

```
SELECT apt_name,
       DECODE(apt_abbr,
              'MCO', 'Going to Disneyworld',
              'MIA', 'CSI Miami, here I come',
              'ATL', 'Need to get some peaches',
              'DFW', 'Everything is bigger in Texas',
              'Is Jacksonville known for anything?')
         AS DC_RETVAL
FROM   airports;

APT_NAME            DC_RETVAL
------------------  ------------------------------------
Orlando, FL         Going to Disneyworld
Atlanta, GA         Need to get some peaches
Miami, FL           CSI Miami, here I come
Jacksonville, FL    Is Jacksonville known for anything?
Dallas/Fort Worth   Everything is bigger in Texas
```

Reporting Aggregated Data Using the Group Functions

Group functions (also known as aggregate functions) return a single result based on multiple rows, as opposed to single-row functions that return one result for each row processed by a given query. Aggregate functions are useful for analyzing data across multiple rows and for locating standout data (like the highest salary or the average age). The data returned might be in multiple groups based on column data if the SELECT statement contains a GROUP BY clause. If there is no GROUP BY clause specified, the complete result returned will be in a single group.

Identify the available group functions

As with the Oracle SQL functions, there are too many group functions available to define them all in this guide. Some of the more common ones follow. For a complete list, you should refer to the SQL Language Reference manual.

AVG
Syntax: AVG(DISTINCT/ALL *expr*)
Purpose: AVG returns average value of *expr*.

```
SELECT AVG(salary) "Average"
FROM   employees;

Average
-------
115814.705882352941176470588235294117647
```

COUNT
Syntax: COUNT(DISTINCT/ALL *expr*)
Purpose: COUNT returns the number of rows where *expr* has at least one non-NULL value.

```
SELECT COUNT(emp_id) "NoNullCount",
       COUNT(afl_id) "CountHasNulls"
FROM   employees;

NoNullCount CountHasNulls
----------- -------------
         17             8
```

The above example demonstrates that the COUNT function will not count individual columns when they contain a NULL value. However, COUNT(*) will count all rows that meet the filter condition even if every single column value is NULL. This is demonstrated with the below example:

```
CREATE TABLE count_null_test (
col1      VARCHAR2(1),
col2      VARCHAR2(1)
);
table COUNT_NULL_TEST created.

INSERT INTO count_null_test VALUES (NULL, NULL);
1 rows inserted.
INSERT INTO count_null_test VALUES (NULL, NULL);
1 rows inserted.
INSERT INTO count_null_test VALUES (NULL, NULL);
1 rows inserted.


SELECT COUNT(*), COUNT(col1), COUNT(col2)
FROM count_null_test;

COUNT(*) COUNT(COL1) COUNT(COL2)
-------- ----------- -----------
       3           0           0
```

MEDIAN
Syntax: MEDIAN(*expr*)
Purpose: MEDIAN takes a numeric or datetime value and returns the middle value or an interpolated value that would be the middle value once the values are sorted.

```
SELECT emp_job, MEDIAN(salary)
FROM employees
GROUP BY emp_job
ORDER BY MEDIAN(salary) DESC;
```

```
EMP_JOB                            MEDIAN(SALARY)
------------------------------     --------------
CEO                                        197500
CFO                                        157000
SVP                                        147150
VP                                         125650
SrDir                                      111000
Mgr                                        101500
Pilot                                       92875
```

MIN
Syntax: MIN(DISTINCT/ALL *expr*)
Purpose: MIN returns minimum value of *expr*.

```
SELECT  MIN(start_date)  "Earliest"
FROM    employees;

Earliest
---------
10-APR-92
```

MAX
Syntax: MAX(DISTINCT/ALL *expr*)
Purpose: MAX returns the maximum value of *expr*.

```
SELECT  MAX(start_date)  "Latest"
FROM    employees;

Latest
---------
07-JUL-04
```

SUM
Syntax: SUM(DISTINCT/ALL *expr*)
Purpose: SUM returns the sum of all expr values.

```
SELECT  SUM(salary)  "Sum_Salary"
FROM    employees;

Sum_Salary
----------
   1935350
```

Describe the use of group functions

Aggregate functions are intended to group together multiple rows based on a supplied common factor and return a single result for the entire group rather than one result for each row in the table. These functions can appear in select lists and in ORDER BY and HAVING clauses. Aggregates are commonly used in conjunction with the GROUP BY clause in a SELECT statement. When a query contains a GROUP BY clause, the individual elements of the select list can be aggregate functions, GROUP BY expressions, constants, or expressions involving one of these. The aggregate functions will be applied to each group of rows and a single result row returned for each group. When a query contains aggregate functions but no GROUP BY clause, the aggregate functions in the select list are applied to all the rows returned by the query. In this event, one row would be returned for the entire statement.

Many aggregate functions that take a single argument will accept the use of the DISTINCT/UNIQUE keyword. These will cause an aggregate function to consider only distinct values of the argument expression. Aggregate functions that will accept DISTINCT/UNIQUE will also accept the ALL keyword. This causes an aggregate function to consider all values, including all duplicates. If you specify no keyword, then the default is ALL. The first example below uses the ALL keyword and the second does not. The results are identical.

```
SELECT COUNT(DISTINCT emp_job) distinct_values, COUNT(ALL
emp_job) AS all_values
FROM  employees;

DISTINCT_VALUES ALL_VALUES
--------------- ----------
              7         17


SELECT COUNT(DISTINCT emp_job) distinct_values,
COUNT(emp_job) AS all_values
FROM  employees;

DISTINCT_VALUES ALL_VALUES
--------------- ----------
              7         17
```

By default NULL values are ignored by all of the aggregate functions. There are exceptions to this rule: the COUNT(*) function as described earlier as well as the GROUPING, and GROUPING_ID aggregate functions. However, for the purposes of the exam, these exceptions are likely to be ignored.

The COUNT function will never <u>return</u> a NULL no matter what the values in the table are. The result of the COUNT function will be an integer value 0 or greater. All other aggregate functions will return a NULL value if a data set either has no rows or has only rows with NULL as the aggregate function argument.

Not all of the aggregate functions can be used against all data types.

- AVG, SUM, MIN, and MAX can be used against numeric data
- MIN and MAX can be used against date data as well
- COUNT can be used against essentially any data

Group data by using the GROUP BY clause

You specify the GROUP BY clause when you want Oracle to group selected rows based on the value of one or more expressions for each row and return a single row of summary information for each group. Expressions in the GROUP BY clause can contain any columns of the tables in the FROM clause, regardless of whether the columns appear in the select list. The GROUP BY clause groups rows but does not guarantee the order of the result set. You must make use of the ORDER BY clause to order the grouped results. When a SELECT clause contains one or more aggregate functions, any column that is not included in a group function must be part of the GROUP BY clause.

```
SELECT emp_job, MAX(salary) max_salary
FROM    employees
GROUP BY emp_job
```

```
EMP_JOB                          MAX_SALARY
-----------------------------    ----------
VP                                   127800
SrDir                                111500
SVP                                  149100
Mgr                                  101500
Pilot                                 98500
CEO                                  197500
CFO                                  157000
```

```
SELECT emp_job, MAX(salary) max_salary
FROM    employees
GROUP BY emp_job
ORDER BY emp_job
```

```
EMP_JOB                          MAX_SALARY
-----------------------------    ----------
CEO                                  197500
CFO                                  157000
Mgr                                  101500
Pilot                                 98500
SVP                                  149100
SrDir                                111500
VP                                   127800
```

When you add additional columns to a GROUP BY clause, you will (generally) increase the number of groups returned by the query. The below examples show data from the AIRCRAFT_FLEET_V view grouped by one column, and then by two columns.

```
SELECT apt_name, SUM(act_seats)
FROM    aircraft_fleet_v
GROUP BY apt_name;
```

```
APT_NAME              SUM(ACT_SEATS)
--------------------  --------------
Miami, FL                        832
Atlanta, GA                      440
Orlando, FL                      700
Dallas/Fort Worth                766
```

```
SELECT apt_name, act_name, SUM(act_seats)
FROM   aircraft_fleet_v
GROUP BY apt_name, act_name;

APT_NAME                  ACT_NAME      SUM(ACT_SEATS)
------------------------- ------------  --------------
Atlanta, GA               Boeing 757               240
Dallas/Fort Worth         Boeing 767               350
Orlando, FL               Boeing 767               700
Atlanta, GA               Boeing 737               200
Miami, FL                 Boeing 747               832
Dallas/Fort Worth         Boeing 747               416
```

Grouping functions can be nested within another grouping function to a limited degree. It's possible to next two levels of grouped functions, but not three. When nesting aggregarte functions the GROUP BY clause is mandatory. In the example below, the average number of seats grouped by the number of decks is calculated.

```
SELECT AVG(act_seats)
FROM   aircraft_types
GROUP BY act_decks;

AVG(ACT_SEATS)
--------------
263.3333333333
           416
```

The SQL from the above query is modified to generate the maximum of the average values returned and completes successfully:

```
SELECT MAX(AVG(act_seats))
FROM   aircraft_types
GROUP BY act_decks;

MAX(AVG(ACT_SEATS))
-------------------
                416
```

The following example attempts to add one more level of nesting and generates an ORA-00935 error:

```
SELECT COUNT(MAX(AVG(act_seats)))
FROM    aircraft_types
GROUP BY act_decks;

SQL Error: ORA-00935: group function is nested too deeply
00935. 00000 -  "group function is nested too deeply"
*Cause:
*Action:
```

Include or exclude grouped rows by using the HAVING clause

When the GROUP BY clause is present in a SQL statement, you can also make use of the HAVING clause. The HAVING clause is used to restrict the groups of returned rows to those groups for which the specified condition is TRUE. If the HAVING clause is omitted, then the database returns summary rows for all groups generated by the query. The GROUP BY and HAVING clauses must be after the WHERE clause and hierarchical query clause (hierarchical queries are discussed later in this guide), but before the ORDER BY clause. If you specify both GROUP BY and HAVING, then they can appear in either order. If a HAVING clause contains a subquery, the subquery is resolved before evaluating the HAVING clause.

If a WHERE clause is included in an aggregate query, it will remove individual rows prior to the aggregation. Always keep in mind that WHERE conditions apply to rows and HAVING conditions apply to groups. Aggregate functions cannot be referenced in the WHERE clause and the HAVING clause cannot filter individual rows.

```
SELECT emp_job, MAX(salary) max_salary
FROM    employees
GROUP BY emp_job
HAVING MAX(salary) > 111500
ORDER BY emp_job

EMP_JOB                              MAX_SALARY
-------------------------------- ----------
CEO                                  197500
CFO                                  157000
SVP                                  149100
VP                                   127800
```

We'll add another filter to the above query to remove the CEO from the results by adding a second condition to the HAVING clause. Since the CEO is a single row in the table, you might expect this to generate an error. However it succeeds and returns the expected results.

```
SELECT emp_job, MAX(salary) max_salary
FROM    employees
GROUP BY emp_job
HAVING MAX(salary) > 111500
AND     emp_job != 'CEO'
ORDER BY emp_job;
```

```
EMP_JOB     MAX_SALARY
---------- ----------
CFO            157000
SVP            149100
VP             127800
```

Filtering the CEO using the WHERE clause also works:

```
SELECT emp_job, MAX(salary) max_salary
FROM    employees
WHERE   emp_job != 'CEO'
GROUP BY emp_job
HAVING MAX(salary) > 111500
ORDER BY emp_job;
```

```
EMP_JOB     MAX_SALARY
---------- ----------
CFO            157000
SVP            149100
VP             127800
```

The reason why this works in either the WHERE or HAVING clauses is because EMP_JOB is part of the GROUP BY clause. Even though only a single row evaluates to 'CEO', the HAVING filter is still removing an entire group. If the HAVING filter were changed to "emp_last != 'Boss'" (which evaluates to the same row in the table), the SELECT statement fails with an error:

```
SELECT emp_job, MAX(salary) max_salary
FROM    employees
GROUP BY emp_job
HAVING MAX(salary) > 111500
AND     emp_last != 'Boss'
ORDER BY emp_job;
```

```
SQL Error: ORA-00979: not a GROUP BY expression
00979. 00000 -  "not a GROUP BY expression"
*Cause:
*Action:
```

When filtering by columns that are not part of the SELECT list, you must use a condition in the WHERE clause:

```
SELECT emp_job, MAX(salary) max_salary
FROM    employees
WHERE   emp_last != 'Boss'
GROUP BY emp_job
HAVING MAX(salary) > 111500
ORDER BY emp_job;

EMP_JOB     MAX_SALARY
---------- ----------
CFO            157000
SVP            149100
VP             127800
```

Displaying Data from Multiple Tables

Any query that combines rows from two or more tables, views, materialized views, subqueries, or table functions must make use of joins (henceforth I'll use the word 'table' to mean any of these). Oracle will perform a join operation any time multiple tables appear in the FROM clause of the query. If multiple tables exist in the FROM clause, the select list can include any columns from any of the tables. When more than one table has a column name in common, then references to duplicated columns must be qualified in all parts of the query (with the exceptions of join columns on NATURAL or JOIN USING joins). You qualify a column name by prefixing it with the table name followed by a period, or with the table alias followed by a period.

The following example joins three tables together: AIRPORTS, AIRCRAFT_FLEET and AIRCRAFT_TYPES. Connecting the three tables requires two join operations. First AIRPORTS is joined to the AIRCRAFT_FLEET table using the APT_ID column that exists in both tables. Second, the AIRCRAFT_FLEET table is joined to the AIRCRAFT_TYPES table by the ACT_ID column that exists in both tables. The AIRPORTS and AIRCRAFT_TYPES tables are not directly joined. The connection between these two tables is through the AIRCRAFT_FLEET table that both are joined to.

```
SELECT apt_name, apt_abbr, act_name, act_seats
FROM   airports apt
       INNER JOIN aircraft_fleet afl
       ON apt.apt_id = afl.apt_id
       INNER JOIN aircraft_types act
       ON act.act_id = afl.act_id
```

APT_NAME	APT_ABBR	ACT_NAME	ACT_SEATS
Orlando, FL	MCO	Boeing 767	350
Orlando, FL	MCO	Boeing 767	350
Atlanta, GA	ATL	Boeing 757	240
Atlanta, GA	ATL	Boeing 737	200
Miami, FL	MIA	Boeing 747	416
Miami, FL	MIA	Boeing 747	416
Dallas/Fort Worth	DFW	Boeing 767	350
Dallas/Fort Worth	DFW	Boeing 747	416

Prior to release 9i, Oracle exclusively used a proprietary join format for connecting tables. With the release of 9i, Oracle began supporting the ANSI standard (SQL:1999) join format. The ANSI style has no performance benefits over the proprietary format. The ANSI style is generally a bit more readable but otherwise contains no real advantage. The ANSI format is the preferred style per Oracle and is what you'll see on the test in any questions containing joins.

The syntax for a join operation using SQL:1999 syntax is:

```
SELECT t1.*, t2.*
FROM    table1 t1
        [NATURAL JOIN table2 t2] |
        [JOIN table2 t2 USING (col_name)] |
        [INNER JOIN table2 t2
         ON (t1.col1 = t2.col2)] |
        [LEFT|RIGHT|FULL OUTER JOIN table2 t2
         ON (t1.col1 = t2.col2)] |
        [CROSS JOIN table2 t2];
```

You should understand the various join definitions.

- **EQUIJOIN** -- A join where the condition contains an equality operator. An equijoin combines rows that have equivalent values for the specified columns.
- **NON-EQUIJOIN** -- A join where the condition does not contain an equality operator – (e.g. the operator might be greater than or less than). A non-equijoin combines rows that have non-equivalent values for the specified columns.
- **SELF-JOIN** -- A join of a table back to itself. The given table will appear twice (or more) in the FROM clause. All incarnations should have table aliases to allow you to qualify column names in the join condition and other parts of the query.
- **INNER JOIN --** An inner join (sometimes called a simple join) is a join of two or more tables that returns only those rows that satisfy the join condition.
- **FULL OUTER JOIN --** An outer join returns all rows that satisfy the join condition and also returns all of those rows from the tables for which no rows from the other satisfy the join condition.
- **LEFT OUTER JOIN –** A left join is a subset of the outer join where all of the rows in the table identified on the left-side of the join

operator are returned and only the rows that meet the join condition are returned from the table on the right side of the operator.

- **RIGHT OUTER JOIN** – A right join is the opposite of the left join. All of the rows in the table identified on the right-side of the join operator are returned and only the rows that meet the join condition are returned from the table on the left side of the operator.
- **CROSS JOIN** -- A cross join is the result when two tables are included in a query but no join condition is specified. When this is the case, Oracle returns the Cartesian product of the two tables (this is sometimes called a Cartesian Join). The Cartesian product is when every row of one table is joined with every row of the other. Generally considered to be useless, cross joins are most often created by mistake.
- **NATURAL JOIN** – A natural join can only be used when the column names and data types used for the join match in both tables. It will perform an inner-equijoin between the two tables.

Note that the above definitions are not exclusive. A join will normally more than one of these definitions at a time. For example, a natural join is always an equijoin and an inner join. A self join is probably an equijoin an inner join as well.

Qualifying column names

When performing a SELECT operation against a single table, there is never any question of what table a given column name in the query belongs to. When multiple tables are joined together, however, it's possible for a query to reference a column name that exists in more than one of the joined tables. When this happens, Oracle must have a means of identifying the correct column. The method by which this is done is called qualifying the column. The table name or table alias is placed in front of the column name followed by a period (i.e. table_name.column_name or table_alias.column_name). It is not required to prefix columns where the table name can be determined by the Oracle SQL parser, but doing so makes the SQL more readable and provides a slight performance improvement during the parse operation.

When a table has been aliased in a query, it is not legal to use the table name as a prefix – you must use the alias. Using the table name will generate an error.

```
SELECT airports.apt_name, airports.apt_abbr
FROM    airports ap;

SQL Error: ORA-00904: "AIRPORTS"."APT_ABBR": invalid
identifier
00904. 00000 -  "%s: invalid identifier"
*Cause:
*Action:
```

If the table is given no alias, then using the full name for a column prefix is legal:

```
SELECT airports.apt_name, airports.apt_abbr
FROM    airports;

APT_NAME                 APT_ABBR
---------------------- --------
Orlando, FL              MCO
Atlanta, GA              ATL
Miami, FL                MIA
Jacksonville, FL         JAX
Dallas/Fort Worth        DFW
```

If the table is given an alias, then you must use the alias (or nothing) as a column prefix:

```
SELECT apt.apt_name, apt_abbr
FROM    airports apt;

APT_NAME                 APT_ABBR
---------------------- --------
Orlando, FL              MCO
Atlanta, GA              ATL
Miami, FL                MIA
Jacksonville, FL         JAX
Dallas/Fort Worth        DFW
```

Write SELECT statements to access data from more than one table using equijoins and nonequijoins

The vast majority of JOIN operations use equijoins. In an equijoin there is a condition such that column A in table one EQUALS column B in table two. In general when there's a need to join two tables, it will be by column data that is exactly equal. The below query uses three equijoins and connects four tables together to generate the required results.

Equijoins

```
SELECT apt_name, act_name, emp_first, emp_last
FROM    airports apt
        INNER JOIN aircraft_fleet afl
        ON apt.apt_id = afl.apt_id
        INNER JOIN aircraft_types act
        ON act.act_id = afl.act_id
        INNER JOIN employees emp
        ON afl.afl_id = emp.afl_id;
```

APT_NAME	ACT_NAME	EMP_FIRST	EMP_LAST
Orlando, FL	Boeing 767	John	Jones
Orlando, FL	Boeing 767	Top	Gun
Atlanta, GA	Boeing 737	Phil	McCoy
Atlanta, GA	Boeing 757	James	Thomas
Miami, FL	Boeing 747	John	Picard
Miami, FL	Boeing 747	Luke	Skytalker
Dallas/Fort Worth	Boeing 747	Dell	Aptop
Dallas/Fort Worth	Boeing 767	Noh	Kia

Because the joins in the above example all are equijoins where the column names match in both tables, the NATURAL JOIN could have been used to generate the same result. If the join column(s) for a NATRUAL JOIN are included anywhere else in the query, they should not be qualified with the table name or alias.

```
SELECT apt_name, act_name, emp_first, emp_last
FROM    airports apt
        NATURAL JOIN aircraft_fleet afl
        NATURAL JOIN aircraft_types act
        NATURAL JOIN employees emp;
```

```
APT_NAME              ACT_NAME       EMP_FIRST    EMP_LAST
--------------------  ------------   -----------  --------------
Orlando, FL           Boeing 767     John         Jones
Orlando, FL           Boeing 767     Top          Gun
Atlanta, GA           Boeing 737     Phil         McCoy
Atlanta, GA           Boeing 757     James        Thomas
Miami, FL             Boeing 747     John         Picard
Miami, FL             Boeing 747     Luke         Skytalker
Dallas/Fort Worth     Boeing 747     Dell         Aptop
Dallas/Fort Worth     Boeing 767     Noh          Kia
```

A third equivalent option for the query is the JOIN...USING syntax. When the USING clause is utilized, only the column name(s) for the JOIN get specified. JOIN..USING is a more flexible means of performing tables with identical column names than a NATURAL join. Just as with a NATURAL JOIN, it is always an EQUIJOIN and the join column names must always be the same in both tables. However, with JOIN...USING, the columns need not be the exact same data type (i.e. one could be CHAR and another VARCHAR or NCHAR). A NATURAL join between two tables will also join by all columns in the two tables that have matching names. The USING clause can specify a subset of columns with matching names. As with a NATURAL join, if the join column(s) are included anywhere else in the query, they should not be qualified with the table name or alias.

```
SELECT apt_name, act_name, emp_first, emp_last
FROM   airports apt
       JOIN aircraft_fleet afl USING (apt_id)
       JOIN aircraft_types act USING (act_id)
       JOIN employees emp USING (afl_id);
```

```
APT_NAME              ACT_NAME       EMP_FIRST    EMP_LAST
--------------------  ------------   -----------  --------------
Orlando, FL           Boeing 767     John         Jones
Orlando, FL           Boeing 767     Top          Gun
Atlanta, GA           Boeing 737     Phil         McCoy
Atlanta, GA           Boeing 757     James        Thomas
Miami, FL             Boeing 747     John         Picard
Miami, FL             Boeing 747     Luke         Skytalker
Dallas/Fort Worth     Boeing 747     Dell         Aptop
Dallas/Fort Worth     Boeing 767     Noh          Kia
```

Finally a fourth syntax option for the query is the JOIN...ON syntax. This is nothing more than the 'INNER JOIN...ON' syntax with the optional 'INNER' left off. However, it's easy to confuse with the JOIN...USING syntax.

When the ON syntax is used, the join condition must specify both columns (qualified if they are the same name) and the operator. If the join columns are in the SELECT list, they must be qualified with the table name or alias.

```
SELECT apt_name, act_name, emp_first, emp_last
FROM   airports apt
       JOIN aircraft_fleet afl ON (apt.apt_id = afl.apt_id)
       JOIN aircraft_types act ON (afl.act_id = act.act_id)
       JOIN employees emp ON (afl.afl_id = emp.afl_id);

APT_NAME                ACT_NAME       EMP_FIRST   EMP_LAST
----------------------- -------------- ----------- -----------
Orlando, FL             Boeing 767     John        Jones
Orlando, FL             Boeing 767     Top         Gun
Atlanta, GA             Boeing 737     Phil        McCoy
Atlanta, GA             Boeing 757     James       Thomas
Miami, FL               Boeing 747     John        Picard
Miami, FL               Boeing 747     Luke        Skytalker
Dallas/Fort Worth       Boeing 747     Dell        Aptop
Dallas/Fort Worth       Boeing 767     Noh         Kia
```

NonEquijoins

On occasion, there is a need to perform a non-equijoin. In a non-equijoin, the condition joining the columns of the two tables uses some condition other than EQUALS. In the below example, the EMPLOYEES table is joined to the SALARY_RANGES table. The join operation uses the BETWEEN operator to find which range each employee's salary falls into in order to determine the salary code.

```
SELECT emp.emp_first, emp.emp_last, salary, slr_code
FROM   employees emp
       INNER JOIN salary_ranges slr
       ON emp.salary BETWEEN slr.slr_lowval
                         AND slr.slr_highval
ORDER BY slr_code DESC;
```

```
EMP_FIRST       EMP_LAST            SALARY SLR_CODE
------------    ------------------  ------ --------
Big             Boss                197500 S09
Adam            Smith               157000 S07
Rob             Stoner              149100 S07
Rick            Jameson             145200 S07
Janet           Jeckson             127800 S06
Bill            Abong               123500 S06
Norm            Storm               101500 S05
Fred            Stoneflint          111500 S05
Alf             Alien               110500 S05
Luke            Skytalker            90000 S04
Dell            Aptop                87500 S04
Phil            McCoy                93500 S04
Noh             Kia                  92250 S04
Top             Gun                  91500 S04
John            Picard               94500 S04
James           Thomas               98500 S04
John            Jones                97500 S04
```

Additional JOIN conditions

You can add additional conditions to the JOIN clause when joining two tables together.

```
SELECT apt_name, act_name, emp_first, emp_last
FROM   airports apt
       JOIN aircraft_fleet afl ON (apt.apt_id = afl.apt_id)
       JOIN aircraft_types act ON (afl.act_id = act.act_id)
                         AND act.act_name='Boeing 767'
       JOIN employees emp ON (afl.afl_id = emp.afl_id);

APT_NAME                 ACT_NAME       EMP_FIRST  EMP_LAST
--------------------     ------------   ---------- ----------
Orlando, FL              Boeing 767     John       Jones
Orlando, FL              Boeing 767     Top        Gun
Dallas/Fort Worth        Boeing 767     Noh        Kia
```

The result of adding this condition to the JOIN clause is indistinguishable from adding the same condition to the WHERE clause.

```
SELECT apt_name, act_name, emp_first, emp_last
FROM   airports apt
       JOIN aircraft_fleet afl ON (apt.apt_id = afl.apt_id)
       JOIN aircraft_types act ON (afl.act_id = act.act_id)
       JOIN employees emp ON (afl.afl_id = emp.afl_id)
WHERE  act.act_name='Boeing 767';
```

APT_NAME	ACT_NAME	EMP_FIRST	EMP_LAST
Orlando, FL	Boeing 767	John	Jones
Orlando, FL	Boeing 767	Top	Gun
Dallas/Fort Worth	Boeing 767	Noh	Kia

Join a table to itself by using a self-join

It's sometimes very useful to join a table back to itself when rows in it reference other rows. In the example below, we join the EMPLOYEES table back to itself by using the EMP_ID and EMP_SUPERVISOR columns. In this fashion we're able to display each employee's manager. Later in this guide, we'll use the CONNECT BY capability to create more complete organization charts.

```
SELECT emp.emp_first, emp.emp_last, mgr.emp_first || ' ' ||
mgr.emp_last AS EMP_MANAGER
FROM    employees emp
        LEFT JOIN employees mgr
        ON emp.emp_supervisor = mgr.emp_id
ORDER BY NVL(mgr.emp_supervisor, 0), emp.emp_last,
emp.emp_first
```

EMP_FIRST	EMP_LAST	EMP_MANAGER
Big	Boss	
Rick	Jameson	Big Boss
Adam	Smith	Big Boss
Rob	Stoner	Big Boss
Bill	Abong	Rick Jameson
Janet	Jeckson	Rob Stoner
Fred	Stoneflint	Bill Abong
Alf	Alien	Janet Jeckson
Norm	Storm	Alf Alien
Dell	Aptop	Norm Storm
Top	Gun	Norm Storm
John	Jones	Norm Storm
Noh	Kia	Norm Storm
Phil	McCoy	Norm Storm
John	Picard	Norm Storm
Luke	Skytalker	Norm Storm
James	Thomas	Norm Storm

View data that generally does not meet a join condition by using outer joins

When you use an INNER join to link two tables where column A of table one equals column B of table two, any rows from both tables that don't meet the specified condition aren't returned by the query. In cases where you would like non-matched rows to be returned, you must use one of the OUTER join syntaxes. There are three varieties of OUTER joins. The behavior of the first two is determined by which side of the join operator a table's column appears on. Using this example:

Table1.Column_A = Table2.Column_B

- **LEFT OUTER JOIN** – Rows from the Table1 will be returned regardless of whether or not there are rows in Table2 where Column_A = Column_B. The 'OUTER' portion of the syntax is optional (i.e. 'LEFT OUTER JOIN' and 'LEFT JOIN' are equivalent)
- **RIGHT OUTER JOIN** – Rows from the Table2 will be returned regardless of whether or not there are rows in Table1 where Column_A = Column_B. The 'OUTER' portion of the syntax is optional (i.e. 'RIGHT OUTER JOIN' and 'RIGHT JOIN' are equivalent)
- **FULL OUTER JOIN** -- Rows from both tables will be returned regardless of whether or not there are rows where Column_A = Column_B.

For the join examples, we'll create the following tables:

```
CREATE TABLE table_A (
   col1      NUMBER,
   col2      VARCHAR2(1)
);

CREATE TABLE table_B (
   col1      NUMBER,
   col2      VARCHAR2(1)
);
```

Now we'll populate them with the below data:

```
INSERT INTO table_A VALUES (1, 'a');
INSERT INTO table_A VALUES (2, 'b');
INSERT INTO table_A VALUES (3, 'c');

INSERT INTO table_B VALUES (2, 'B');
INSERT INTO table_B VALUES (3, 'C');
INSERT INTO table_B VALUES (4, 'D');
```

An INNER JOIN between these two tables produces the following results:

```
SELECT a.col1, a.col2, b.col2
FROM   table_A a
       INNER JOIN table_B b
       ON a.col1 = b.col1;

COL1 COL2 COL2
---- ---- ----
   2 b    B
   3 c    C
```

Changing to a LEFT JOIN produces the results below. The row in table_A without a matching value in table_B is now displayed. The LEFT JOIN will return rows without matches from the table represented on the left side of the JOIN operator (in this case a.col1).

```
SELECT a.col1, a.col2, b.col2
FROM   table_A a
       LEFT JOIN table_B b
       ON a.col1 = b.col1;

COL1 COL2 COL2
---- ---- ----
   2 b    B
   3 c    C
   1 a
```

Changing to a RIGHT JOIN produces the results below. Now the row in table_B without a matching value in table_A is now displayed. The RIGHT JOIN will return rows without matches from the table represented on the right side of the JOIN operator (in this case b.col1). We could have gotten the same results by continuing to use the LEFT JOIN but reversing the join condition order (i.e. b.col1 = a.col1).

```
SELECT a.col1, a.col2, b.col2
FROM  table_A a
      RIGHT JOIN table_B b
      ON a.col1 = b.col1;

COL1 COL2 COL2
---- ---- ----
   2 b    B
   3 c    C
          D
```

Changing to a FULL OUTER JOIN produces the results below. In this case, all rows in both tables are returned regardless of whether the condition evaluates to TRUE.

```
SELECT a.col1, a.col2, b.col2
FROM  table_A a
      FULL OUTER JOIN table_B b
      ON a.col1 = b.col1;

COL1 COL2 COL2
---- ---- ----
   2 b    B
   3 c    C
          D
   1 a
```

Generate a Cartesian product of all rows from two or more tables

A Cartesian product, or CROSS JOIN between two tables is something that is generally created by accident. The result of this operation is that every single row of the first table is joined to every single row of the second. The result if either or both of the tables contain many rows can be enormous (the multiple of the rows in the first table times the rows in the second). A Cartesian JOIN between the AIRPORTS table (5 rows) and the AIRCRAFT_TYPES table (4 rows) creates a result with 20 rows. The example below is sorted by the airport and then the aircraft type to highlight the way the rows in these two tables have been joined.

```
SELECT apt_name, apt_abbr, act_name, act_seats
FROM    airports apt
        CROSS JOIN aircraft_types act
ORDER BY apt_name, act_name;
```

```
APT_NAME                 APT_ABBR ACT_NAME      ACT_SEATS
----------------------   -------- ------------  ---------
Atlanta, GA              ATL      Boeing 737          200
Atlanta, GA              ATL      Boeing 747          416
Atlanta, GA              ATL      Boeing 757          240
Atlanta, GA              ATL      Boeing 767          350
Dallas/Fort Worth        DFW      Boeing 737          200
Dallas/Fort Worth        DFW      Boeing 747          416
Dallas/Fort Worth        DFW      Boeing 757          240
Dallas/Fort Worth        DFW      Boeing 767          350
Jacksonville, FL         JAX      Boeing 737          200
Jacksonville, FL         JAX      Boeing 747          416
Jacksonville, FL         JAX      Boeing 757          240
Jacksonville, FL         JAX      Boeing 767          350
Miami, FL                MIA      Boeing 737          200
Miami, FL                MIA      Boeing 747          416
Miami, FL                MIA      Boeing 757          240
Miami, FL                MIA      Boeing 767          350
Orlando, FL              MCO      Boeing 737          200
Orlando, FL              MCO      Boeing 747          416
Orlando, FL              MCO      Boeing 757          240
Orlando, FL              MCO      Boeing 767          350
```

The below query would generate results identical to the above one. Since no join condition is specified, Oracle has no alternative but to joins all rows in both tables. A Cartesian product will also result if a join condition is specified, but invalid (assuming the invalid condition is not one that causes the SQL statement to fail altogether).

```
SELECT apt_name, apt_abbr, act_name, act_seats
FROM   airports apt,
       aircraft_types act
ORDER BY apt_name, act_name;
```

Using Subqueries to Solve Queries

Subqueries are generally used to answer questions that contain multiple parts. For example, you might have a need to determine which pilots fly the same type of aircraft as James Thomas. To determine that, it is first necessary to determine which aircraft James pilots. Once the answer to that is located, a second query is required to find out what other pilots fly that same aircraft. This question can be answered by a single select statement that contains an inner query (subquery) that finds James' aircraft and an outer query (parent query) that uses the results of the subquery to filter for pilots with the same aircraft. With the exception of correlated queries, subqueries will always execute before the parent query and the results of the subquery will then be passed to the parent to be used in its execution.

- **Inline View**: A subquery in the FROM clause of a SELECT statement. It possible to nest any number of subqueries in an inline view.
- **Nested Subquery**: A subquery in the WHERE clause of a SELECT statement. You can nest up to 255 levels of subqueries in a nested subquery.

If columns in a subquery have the same name as columns in the outer query and columns from the outer query are referenced in the subquery, then column references are required. You must prefix all references to the column of the table from the containing statement with the table name or alias. It's good practice to prefix the subquery column references as well, but not a requirement.

```
SELECT emp_first, emp_last, emp_job
FROM    employees emp
WHERE   salary > (SELECT slr_highval
                  FROM    salary_ranges
                  WHERE   slr_code = 'S05')
```

```
EMP_FIRST   EMP_LAST    EMP_JOB
----------  ----------  ----------
Big         Boss        CEO
Adam        Smith       CFO
Rick        Jameson     SVP
Rob         Stoner      SVP
Bill        Abong       VP
Janet       Jeckson     VP
```

Define subqueries

A subquery is a query that is nested inside another query. The outer query might be a SELECT, INSERT, UPDATE, or DELETE statement (or another subquery). Subqueries can return a single row or multiple rows; a single column or multiple columns. A subquery generally executes first and its result then used as part of the outer query. The exception to this is a correlated query which will be discussed later in this section. A subquery can be used in any of the following locations:

- The SELECT list
  ```
  SELECT col1, col2, (SELECT expr FROM table) as sqexp
  FROM    table_name;
  ```

- The FROM clause
  ```
  SELECT col1, col2, col3
  FROM    (SELECT col1, col2, col3
           FROM    table_name);
  ```

- The WHERE clause
  ```
  SELECT col1, col2, col3
  FROM    table_name
  WHERE col1 = (SELECT col1
               FROM table_name2);
  ```

- The HAVING clause
  ```
  SELECT col1, col2, SUM(col3)
  FROM    table_name1
  GROUP BY col1, col2
  HAVING SUM(col3) = (SELECT expr
                     FROM table_name2);
  ```

Describe the types of problems that the subqueries can solve

There are several ways in which subqueries can be utilized.

Create a Table Equivalent to SELECT From

A subquery can be used in the FROM clause of a query as a table-equivalent. When used in this fashion, they are called inline views. The subquery is used to format the table data in a fashion that makes it possible for the outer SELECT to return the desired results. Inline views often aggregate data from the base table.

```
SELECT emp_job, avg_sal, min_sal || ' - ' ||  max_sal AS
salary_range
FROM   (SELECT emp_job, AVG(salary) AVG_SAL, MIN(salary)
MIN_SAL, MAX(salary) MAX_SAL
       FROM    employees
       GROUP BY emp_job)
ORDER BY max_sal DESC

EMP_JOB      AVG_SAL SALARY_RANGE
---------- ------- -----------------
CEO           197500 197500 - 197500
CFO           157000 157000 - 157000
SVP           147150 145200 - 149100
VP            125650 123500 - 127800
SrDir         111000 110500 - 111500
Mgr           101500 101500 - 101500
Pilot       93156.25 87500 - 98500
```

Generate a Result Set to Filter by

You might use a subquery to answer questions such as which airports have 747s based at them. You could answer that with a subquery such as the below example.

```
SELECT apt_name, apt_abbr
FROM   airports apt
WHERE  apt.apt_id IN (SELECT apt_id
                      FROM   aircraft_types act
                             INNER JOIN aircraft_fleet afl
                             ON act.act_id = afl.act_id
                      WHERE  act_name = 'Boeing 747')
```

```
APT_NAME                    APT_ABBR
--------------------        --------
Miami, FL                   MIA
Dallas/Fort Worth           DFW
```

Generate Projection Columns

When utilized in the SELECT list of a query, scalar subqueries act like SQL functions to generate new expressions.

```
SELECT emp_first, emp_last, salary,
       (SELECT AVG(salary)
        FROM    employees
        WHERE   emp_job='Pilot') AVG_SALARY
FROM    employees
WHERE   emp_job = 'Pilot';
```

```
EMP_FIRST  EMP_LAST    SALARY  AVG_SALARY
---------  ----------  ------  ----------
John       Jones        97500    88968.75
Top        Gun          91500    88968.75
Phil       McCoy       105000    88968.75
James      Thomas       98500    88968.75
John       Picard       49500    88968.75
Luke       Skytalker    90000    88968.75
Dell       Aptop        87500    88968.75
Noh        Kia          92250    88968.75
```

Generate Data for an INSERT, UPDATE, or DELETE

A subquery can be used to generate a set of rows to be inserted into a table. Alternately, a scalar subquery could be utilized as the source expression for an update statement. Finally, a subquery could be used to identify rows that meet a given criteria and pass the result to a delete statement.

This statement would add a new row into the AIRCRAFT_TYPES table for the Boeing 787, pulling some values from the 767. It does not supply a primary key value, so if there were not a trigger in place to provide that data, the INSERT would fail.

```
INSERT INTO aircraft_types (act_name, act_body_style,
act_decks, act_seats)
SELECT 'Boeing 787', act_body_style, act_decks, 300
FROM    aircraft_types
WHERE   act_name = 'Boeing 767';
```

When using a subquery in an INSERT statement insert data into a table, the VALUES clause is not used. A subquery inside a VALUES clause is illegal and will generate an error. The reverse is also true. An INSERT that is not using a subquery must have the VALUES keyword.

This statement would move all aircraft based in Orlando to Dallas/Ft Worth:

```
UPDATE aircraft_fleet
SET    apt_id = (SELECT apt_id
                 FROM   airports
                 WHERE  apt_abbr = 'DFW')
WHERE  apt_id = (SELECT apt_id
                 FROM   airports
                 WHERE  apt_abbr = 'MCO');
```

This statement would delete any rows from the AIRCRAFT_TYPES table if there is not currently an aircraft of that type in the fleet.

```
DELETE FROM aircraft_types
WHERE  act_id NOT IN (SELECT act_id
                      FROM   aircraft_fleet);
```

List the types of subqueries

At the highest level, there are three classes of subqueries:

- **Single-row subqueries** – A single-row subquery returns a single result row to the parent SQL. When only a single column is returned, it is a special subclass called a scalar subquery. Scalar subqueries can be used in almost every location where you can use an expression, literal value, or a constant.
- **Multiple-row subqueries** -- A multiple-row subquery returns result sets with more than one row to the surrounding SQL. Often they are used to generate results for a SELECT statement or DML statement.
- **Correlated subqueries** – When a subquery references column data from the parent query, the results become dependent on the parent. Since the parent data can change with each row returned by the parent query, unlike a single or multiple-row subquery that

run a single time when a SQL statement is executed, a correlated subquery must run once for each row of the parent. The results can be useful, but correlated subqueries can create performance problems depending on the execute time of the subquery and the number of rows evaluated in the parent query.

Write single-row and multiple-row subqueries

Following are some examples of single- and multiple-row subqueries. While either type of subquery may be used in the WHERE and HAVING clauses of the parent query, you must use a valid comparison operator. The two lists below show valid operators for single and multiple row subqueries. It's important to note that while multiple-row operators will work correctly if only a single row is returned by a subquery, the reverse is not true. Single row operators will generate an error if more than one row is returned.

Single Row Operators
- = -- Equal to
- > -- Greater than
- >= -- Greater than or equal to
- < -- Less than
- <= -- Less than or equal to
- <> or != -- Not equal to

Multiple Row Operators
- **IN** -- Equal to any member in a list
- **NOT IN** -- Not equal to any member in a list
- **ANY** -- TRUE when any rows match the comparison value. Must be preceded by <, >, <=, >=, =, or !=.
- **ALL** – TRUE when all rows match the comparison value. Must be preceded by <, >, <=, >=, =, or !=.
- **EXISTS** -- TRUE when the subquery returns any rows
- **NOT EXISTS** -- TRUE when the subquery returns no rows

Single-Row Subquery

The following example has a subquery that pulls the aircraft fleet record for the pilot named Picard. That information is used in the outer query to pull in information about that aircraft.

```
SELECT apt_name, apt_abbr, act_name, act_seats
FROM   airports apt
       INNER JOIN aircraft_fleet afl
       ON apt.apt_id = afl.apt_id
       INNER JOIN aircraft_types act
       ON act.act_id = afl.act_id
WHERE  afl_id = (SELECT afl_id
                 FROM    employees
                 WHERE   emp_last = 'Picard')

APT_NAME                    APT_ABBR ACT_NAME       ACT_SEATS
--------------------        -------- ------------   ---------
Miami, FL                   MIA      Boeing 747          416
```

Multiple-Row Subquery

In this example, the only changes are the addition of two more pilots and a change in the operator used for the subquery comparison. The '=' operator has been replaced by the 'IN' operator. The remainder of the query is identical and the result is information about three aircraft instead of one. The previous example could have used the 'IN' operator instead of the '=' operator with no change in functionality.

```
SELECT apt_name, apt_abbr, act_name, act_seats
FROM   airports apt
       INNER JOIN aircraft_fleet afl
       ON apt.apt_id = afl.apt_id
       INNER JOIN aircraft_types act
       ON act.act_id = afl.act_id
WHERE  afl_id IN (SELECT afl_id
                  FROM    employees
                  WHERE   emp_last IN ('Picard', 'McCoy', 'Aptop')
                  )

APT_NAME                    APT_ABBR ACT_NAME       ACT_SEATS
--------------------        -------- ------------   ---------
Atlanta, GA                 ATL      Boeing 737          200
Miami, FL                   MIA      Boeing 747          416
Dallas/Fort Worth           DFW      Boeing 747          416
```

- Subqueries can include GROUP functions as part of their syntax.
- Subqueries cannot include an ORDER BY clause.
- Subqueries that return no rows evaluate to NULL

Using the Set Operators

Set operators allow you to combine the results from two or more SELECT statements. The results of individual SELECT statements are treated as sets, and SQL set operations are applied against the sets to generate the desired result. Queries joined by set operators are also known as compound queries.

Describe set operators

Oracle supports the following set operations:

- **UNION** – Combines the results of two SELECT operations into a single set. Duplicate rows are removed from the end result.
- **UNION ALL** -- Combines the results of two SELECT operations into a single set. Duplicate rows are included in the end result.
- **INTERSECT** – Returns distinct rows where all selected values exist in both queries.
- **MINUS** – Returns distinct rows selected by the first query but not the second.

All set operators have equal precedence. Any time a SQL statement contains multiple set operators, Oracle will evaluate them from top to bottom unless parentheses are used to explicitly specify a different order. The select lists of every query being combined with SET operators must have the same number of columns and each column position must be in the same data type group. For example, column one in the first SELECT could be a VARCHAR2 field and column one in the second SELECT a CHAR field. However, if column one in the first query is a VARCHAR2 field and column one in the second query is a NUMBER field, Oracle will generate an error. It is also possible to use SET operators in subqueries.

Columns names returned by the query are determined by the first SELECT statement. An ORDER BY clause can only be placed at the very end of a compound query involving set operators.

Restrictions on the Set Operators
- Set operations cannot be performed on BLOB, CLOB, BFILE, VARRAY, or nested table columns.
- UNION, INTERSECT, and MINUS operators are not valid on LONG columns.
- Expressions in the SELECT list must have an alias in order to be used in the order_by clause.
- Set operators cannot be used with the for_update_clause.
- Set operations are not allowed on SELECT statements containing TABLE collection expressions.

Use a set operator to combine multiple queries into a single query

Following are examples of each of the four types of SET operations. For the examples, we'll use the following tables and data:

```
CREATE TABLE table_setA (
  col1      VARCHAR2(1)
);

CREATE TABLE table_setB (
  col1      VARCHAR2(1)
);

INSERT INTO table_setA VALUES ('A');
INSERT INTO table_setA VALUES ('A');
INSERT INTO table_setA VALUES ('A');
INSERT INTO table_setA VALUES ('A');
INSERT INTO table_setA VALUES ('B');
INSERT INTO table_setA VALUES ('C');

INSERT INTO table_setB VALUES ('B');
INSERT INTO table_setB VALUES ('B');
INSERT INTO table_setB VALUES ('C');
INSERT INTO table_setB VALUES ('C');
INSERT INTO table_setB VALUES ('D');
INSERT INTO table_setB VALUES ('D');
INSERT INTO table_setB VALUES ('D');
```

If the UNION set operator is used to combine results from these two tables, it will produce the distinct values returned by the two queries:

```
SELECT col1
FROM    table_setA
UNION
SELECT col1
FROM    table_setB

COL1
----
A
B
C
D
```

If the UNION ALL set operator is used to combine results from these two tables, it will produce all values returned by the two queries. The UNION ALL is the only set operator that does not produce distinct results.

```
SELECT col1
FROM    table_setA
UNION ALL
SELECT col1
FROM    table_setB;

COL1
----
A
A
A
A
B
C
B
B
C
C
D
D
D
```

If the INTERSECT set operator is used to combine results from these two tables, it will produce only values returned by both queries.

```
SELECT  col1
FROM    table_setA
INTERSECT
SELECT  col1
FROM    table_setB;

COL1
----
B
C
```

If the MINUS set operator is used to combine results from these two tables, it will produce only values returned by the first query, but not the second. MINUS is the only set operator where the order of the queries will change the results.

```
SELECT  col1
FROM    table_setA
MINUS
SELECT  col1
FROM    table_setB;

COL1
----
A


SELECT  col1
FROM    table_setB
MINUS
SELECT  col1
FROM    table_setA;

COL1
----
D
```

Control the order of rows returned

By default, the output of compound queries is not sorted. The output of the individual sets will be returned in groups, and the sorting within the groups is largely indeterminate. It is not allowable to make use of ORDER BY clauses in the individual queries. To sort the results of a compound query, you must place an ORDER BY clause at the end of the statement.

This will sort the entire output of the compound query. With compound queries, making use of column position to sort by is often useful. The individual column names of the components may be different. If you use column names or aliases, you must use them from the first SELECT list in the compound query.

The following example orders rows returned from the EMPLOYEES table by the employee's last name, then by their first name. The columns are specified by name.

```
SELECT emp_last, emp_first, salary, start_date
FROM    employees
WHERE   emp_job = 'Pilot'
ORDER BY emp_last, emp_first

EMP_LAST   EMP_FIRST  SALARY START_DATE
---------- ---------- ------ ----------
Aptop      Dell        87500 22-AUG-03
Gun        Top         91500 13-OCT-96
Jones      John        97500 10-APR-95
Kia        Noh         92250 07-JUL-04
McCoy      Phil        93500 09-JUN-96
Picard     John        94500 11-NOV-01
Skytalker  Luke        90000 10-SEP-02
Thomas     James       98500 12-MAY-99
```

The following example orders rows returned from the EMPLOYEES table by the start date. The column is specified by position.

```
SELECT emp_last, emp_first, salary, start_date
FROM    employees
WHERE   emp_job = 'Pilot'
ORDER BY 4

EMP_LAST   EMP_FIRST  SALARY START_DATE
---------- ---------- ------ ----------
Jones      John        97500 10-APR-95
McCoy      Phil        93500 09-JUN-96
Gun        Top         91500 13-OCT-96
Thomas     James       98500 12-MAY-99
Picard     John        94500 11-NOV-01
Skytalker  Luke        90000 10-SEP-02
Aptop      Dell        87500 22-AUG-03
Kia        Noh         92250 07-JUL-04
```

Manipulating Data

Data Manipulation Language (DML) is the name given to the SQL statements used to manage data in the Oracle database. DML statements include INSERT, UPDATE, DELETE and MERGE. The SELECT statement could technically be considered a DML statement but is seldom considered one in practice. As a general rule, only commands which add, alter, or remove rows from database tables are considered to be data manipulation statements. However, if SELECT is not included with DML, then it has no place to be. It is certainly not Data Definition Language (DDL) or Data Control Language (DCL). Just be aware that when reference is made to DML statements, the context probably does not include SELECT operations.

Describe each data manipulation language (DML) statement

Data manipulation language statements are utilized to manage data in existing schema objects. DML statements do not modify information in the data dictionary and do not implicitly commit the current transaction. The most commonly identified DML commands are:

- **INSERT** – Used to populate data in tables. It is possible to insert one row into one table, one row into multiple tables, multiple rows into one table, or multiple rows into multiple tables.
- **UPDATE** – Used to alter data that already been inserted into a database table. An UPDATE can affect a single row or multiple rows, a single column or multiple columns. The WHERE clause will determine which rows in the table are altered. A single UPDATE statement can only act on a single table.
- **DELETE** – Used to remove previously inserted rows from a table. The command can remove a single row or multiple rows from a table. When executed with no WHERE clause, it will remove all rows from the target table. It is not possible to delete individual columns – the entire row is deleted or it is not.
- **MERGE** – Used for hybrid DML operations. The MERGE can insert, update and delete rows in a table all in a single statement. There

is no operation that a MERGE can perform that could not be performed by a combination of INSERT, UPDATE and DELETE.

Insert rows into a table

You can add new rows to an Oracle table with the INSERT statement. The syntax of a single table INSERT is:

```
INSERT INTO table_name [(column [,column...])]
VALUES (value [, value...]);
```

In this statement, table_name is the table into which rows will be inserted, column is the name of the column of the table values are being added to, and value is the data that will be inserted into the column. The column list is optional, but if omitted, the values clause must include all columns of the table in the order that they are recorded in the Oracle data dictionary. A column list allows you to insert into a subset of the table columns and explicitly match the order of the columns to the order of the values list. When there are multiple rows or columns, they are enclosed by parentheses and separated by commas.

The simplest form of an insert statement inserts a single row into a single table. The following inserts a new person into the EMPLOYEES table (described below).

```
desc employees
Name             Null        Type
-------------    --------    ------------
EMP_ID           NOT NULL    NUMBER
AFL_ID                       NUMBER
EMP_FIRST                    VARCHAR2(10)
EMP_LAST         NOT NULL    VARCHAR2(10)
EMP_JOB                      VARCHAR2(10)
EMP_SUPERVISOR               NUMBER
SALARY                       NUMBER
START_DATE                   DATE
```

```
INSERT INTO employees (emp_id, afl_id, emp_first, emp_last,
emp_job,
                     emp_supervisor, salary, start_date)
VALUES (18, NULL, 'Guy', 'Newberry', 'Mgr', 8, 98250, '07-
JAN-2012');
```

Note that character data is enclosed by quotes as is the one date field. Numeric values being inserted into a NUMBER column are not generally enclosed by quotes, but it will not generate an error if you do (Oracle will implicitly convert the value back to a number data type during the INSERT operation). The NULL keyword cannot be enclosed in quotes. If it were, instead of a NULL value being inserted, the text 'NULL' would be inserted (or an error generated if the column were not a character field)..

The above INSERT statement contains all of the values of the EMPLOYEES table and the column order matches that in the data dictionary. The column list is therefore optional and the INSERT can be performed like this:

```
INSERT INTO employees
VALUES (18, NULL, 'Guy', 'Newberry', 'Mgr', 8, 98250,
       '07-JAN-2012');
```

To insert into only a subset of columns in a table, you must provide a list of the columns that you wish to provide values for. Any columns not provided in the column list will contain a NULL after the INSERT operation unless they have a default value or are populated by a trigger. The following statement would insert a row into the employees table, leaving the SALARY and START_DATE fields NULL. Note that if either of the columns had a NOT NULL constraint, then the statement would fail.

```
INSERT INTO employees (emp_id, afl_id, emp_first, emp_last,
                     emp_job, emp_supervisor)
VALUES (18, NULL, 'Guy', 'Newberry', 'Mgr', 8);
```

The same operation could have been performed without a column list by explicitly adding the NULL values to the INSERT statement:

```
INSERT INTO employees
VALUES (18, NULL, 'Guy', 'Newberry', 'Mgr', 8, NULL, NULL);
```

DEFAULT column values

If a column in the table that is being inserted into contains a DEFAULT value, you can make use of that value by using DEFAULT in your VALUES clause. In the example below, a DEFAULT is added to the start_date field such that is will use the current system date. An insert is then performed explicitly using DEFAULT as the value for the START_DATE column:

```
ALTER TABLE employees MODIFY(start_date DEFAULT SYSDATE);
table EMPLOYEES altered.

INSERT INTO employees (emp_id, afl_id, emp_first, emp_last,
                       emp_job, emp_supervisor, salary,
                       start_date)
VALUES (18, NULL, 'Guy', 'Newberry', 'Mgr', 8, 90000,
DEFAULT);
1 rows inserted.

SELECT emp_first, emp_last,  start_date
FROM   employees
WHERE  emp_last='Newberry';

EMP_FIRST  EMP_LAST   START_DATE
---------- ---------- ----------
Guy        Newberry   11-APR-12
```

Instead of using the DEFAULT keyword, the INSERT could have simply ignored the START_DATE column such as the below example:

```
INSERT INTO employees (emp_id, afl_id, emp_first, emp_last,
                       emp_job, emp_supervisor, salary)
VALUES (18, NULL, 'Guy', 'Newberry', 'Mgr', 8, 90000);
1 rows inserted.

SELECT emp_first, emp_last,  start_date
FROM   employees
WHERE  emp_last='Newberry';

EMP_FIRST  EMP_LAST   START_DATE
---------- ---------- ----------
Guy        Newberry   11-APR-12
```

However, if the field is included in the INSERT and VALUES clauses and a NULL is explicitly inserted, then this will override the DEFAULT value of the column:

```
INSERT INTO employees (emp_id, afl_id, emp_first, emp_last,
                       emp_job, emp_supervisor, salary,
                       start_date)
VALUES (18, NULL, 'Guy', 'Newberry', 'Mgr', 8, 90000, NULL);
1 rows inserted.

SELECT emp_first, emp_last,  start_date
FROM   employees
WHERE  emp_last='Newberry';

EMP_FIRST  EMP_LAST   START_DATE
---------- ---------- ----------
Guy        Newberry
```

Insert using subquery

In lieu of providing values explicitly for an INSERT statement, it's possible to generate data through a SELECT statement. The following operation inserts a row into the AIRCRAFT_TYPES table using a subquery against the same table. A subquery used for such an operation can be against any table that will produce the data required. When inserting using a subquery, the VALUES keyword is not used. The number and order of columns returned by the subquery must match the number and order of columns in the INSERT statement.

```
INSERT INTO aircraft_types (act_name, act_body_style,
act_decks, act_seats)
SELECT 'Boeing 787', act_body_style, act_decks, 300
FROM   aircraft_types
```

Update rows in a table

An UPDATE operation is used to modify existing data in a table. You can update a single row in a table, multiple rows using a filter, or the entire table. If an update does not contain a WHERE clause, every single row in the target table will be updated. The syntax for an UPDATE is:

```
UPDATE table_name
SET    column1 = value1 [, column2 = value2, …]
[WHERE condition];
```

The following statement moves all of the employees that used to report to the employees with emp_id 9 to the new employee with emp_id 18. If no WHERE clause were supplied, all rows in the employees table would have the emp_supervisor field set to 18.

```
UPDATE employees
SET    emp_supervisor = 18
WHERE  emp_supervisor = 9;
```

As with the INSERT statement, it's possible to use a subquery to provide the data used for an UPDATE operation. T the column count and order must match between the UPDATE and results generated by the subquery. The syntax for this is:

```
UPDATE table_name
SET    (column1 [, column2 …] = (SELECT column1 [, column2 …]
FROM sqtab)
[WHERE condition];
```

Delete rows from a table

The DELETE operation removes rows that already exist in a table. The syntax for a DELETE statement is:

```
DELETE
[FROM] table_name
[WHERE condition];
```

Only the keyword DELETE and a table name are required. If you issue the command 'DELETE employees', then all rows in the EMPLOYEES table will be deleted. The FROM keyword is seldom left off of DELETE statements in practice, but it is strictly optional. The following statement deletes from the EMPLOYEES table the employee with emp_id 9.

```
DELETE
FROM    employees
WHERE   emp_id = 9;
```

There is no data to be supplied for a DELETE operation as there is with INSERT and UPDATE operations. However, it's possible to use a subquery in the WHERE clause to dynamically build the filter of rows to be deleted.

An alternative to the DELETE statement is TRUNCATE. The TRUNCATE command is not a DML operation, but rather a DDL operation. DDL operations perform implicit commits, so unlike a DELETE statement, a TRUNCATE cannot simply be rolled back if it was performed in error. The syntax of a TRUNCATE is:

```
TRUNCATE TABLE table_name;
```

The TRUNCATE operation will remove all rows from the table it is executed against. There is no way to apply a filter to restrict what rows are removed. It is, however, much faster and efficient of database resources than a DELETE statement. Because it does not generate ROLLBACK data or fire DELETE triggers, it generates much less overhead. If a table contains the parent key of a foreign key constraint, it is not possible to TRUNCATE the table while the constraint is enabled. There are other benefits to using a TRUNCATE operation, but they are outside the scope of the exam (in fact TRUNCATE itself probably won't be).

Control transactions

A transaction is composed of one or more DML statements punctuated by either a COMMIT or a ROLLBACK command. Transactions are a major part of the mechanism for ensuring the database maintains data integrity. The transaction control statements available in Oracle follow. However, only the first three of the above TCL statements are liable to appear on the exam.

- **COMMIT** – Used to end the current transaction and make permanent all changes performed in it.
- **ROLLBACK** -- Used to undo work done in the current transaction or to manually undo the work done by an in-doubt distributed transaction.
- **SAVEPOINT** -- Used to create a name for a specific system change number (SCN), which can be rolled back to at a later date.

- **SET TRANSACTION** – Used to establish the current transaction as read-only or read/write, establish its isolation level, assign it to a specified rollback segment, or assign a name to it.
- **SET CONSTRAINT** -- Used to specify, for a particular transaction, whether a deferrable constraint is checked following each DML statement (IMMEDIATE) or when the transaction is committed (DEFERRED).

A transaction begins when an initial DML statement is issued against the database. This can be followed by any number of additional DML statements. The transaction will continue until one of the following events occurs:

- A COMMIT or ROLLBACK statement is issued
- A DDL statement is issued (DDL statements issue an implicit COMMIT)
- The user exits SQL*Plus or SQL Developer
- SQL*Plus or SQL Developer terminates abnormally.
- The database shuts down abnormally (a crash or shutdown abort).

When performing DML operations, if transaction control is left to only the COMMIT and ROLLBACK commands, the only options to complete a transaction are to accept everything that has been changed and make the changes permanent or accept nothing and undo everything since the last COMMIT. The SAVEPOINT transaction control statement of Oracle allows there to be a middle ground between the two. With savepoints, you can identify specific locations within the transaction that you can go back to – undoing any DML statements later than that point, but leaving intact all the ones prior to it. The example below shows an example of savepoints.

```
COMMIT;
INSERT INTO employees (emp_id, afl_id, emp_first, emp_last,
                       emp_job, emp_supervisor)
VALUES (30, NULL, 'Adam', 'Apple', 'Pilot', 9);

INSERT INTO employees (emp_id, afl_id, emp_first, emp_last,
                       emp_job, emp_supervisor)
VALUES (31, NULL, 'Bob', 'Hopeful', 'Pilot', 9);

SAVEPOINT A;
```

```
INSERT INTO employees (emp_id, afl_id, emp_first, emp_last,
                       emp_job, emp_supervisor)
VALUES (32, NULL, 'Charlie', 'Chafing', 'Pilot', 9);

INSERT INTO employees (emp_id, afl_id, emp_first, emp_last,
                       emp_job, emp_supervisor)
VALUES (33, NULL, 'Dude', 'Whersmicar', 'Pilot', 9);

SAVEPOINT B;

INSERT INTO employees (emp_id, afl_id, emp_first, emp_last,
                       emp_job, emp_supervisor)
VALUES (33, NULL, 'Ed', 'Horse', 'Pilot', 9);
```

There are three places that this transaction can be rolled back to.

- **ROLLBACK TO SAVEPOINT B** – Will undo only the last INSERT statement.
- **ROLLBACK TO SAVEPOINT A** – Will undo the last three INSERT statements.
- **ROLLBACK** – Will undo all five INSERT statements.

Note that any DDL operations will end a transaction immediately with an implicit commit. Any SAVEPOINT prior to that operation can no longer be rolled back to. Also, if within the same transaction you reuse a savepoint name, then any ROLLBACK to that savepoint will only undo to the latest one of that name – the earlier one of that name is deleted automatically when the newer one is created..

Uncommited Transactions

Uncommitted transactions in Oracle are in limbo – it's not certain whether they will ever be permanent and so there is limited access to them. Because they might be reversed, the data required to do so must be retained in the rollback segment indefinitely until the changes are either committed or rolled back. Pending transactions have the following four characteristics:

- The changed data is visible to the user that issued the DML.
- The changed data is NOT visible to any other user.
- The rows with the changed data are locked and cannot be altered by any other user.
- The data prior to the DML can be recovered by rolling back the transaction.

Committed Transactions

Committed transactions in Oracle have been made permanent (although obviously they can be changed with another DML operation). Since they have been made permanent, the portion of the rollback segment holding the prior data is released, and the changed rows made accessible. Committed transactions have the following four characteristics:

- The changed data is visible to all database users.
- The locks on the rows affected by the DML are released and they can be updated.
- The changed data has been made permanent and cannot be reversed with a ROLLBACK.
- Any SAVEPOINTs from the transaction are deleted.

If a DML statement fails due to an error, a constraint violation or some other cause, Oracle will roll the statement back. If there are earlier uncommitted DML operations that succeeded without error, they will not be affected by the rollback of the failed statement. If the failed statement is reason to reverse the earlier DML statements, you can issue an explicit rollback. If the statement can be repaired, then you can fix the failed statement and continue on with the remaining portion of the transaction without having to re-issue the preceding DML operations.

Using DDL Statements to Create and Manage Tables

Whereas DML statements are used to manipulate data, data definition language (DDL) statements are used to make changes to the data dictionary of Oracle.   They are utilized to perform the following tasks (among others):

- Create, alter, and drop schema objects
- Grant and revoke privileges and roles
- Analyze information on a table, index, or cluster

Categorize the main database objects

There are over thirty different types of objects that make up the Oracle database. The list of database objects, both schema and nonschema from the 11G SQL Reference manual follows.

Schema Objects
Clusters
Constraints
Database links
Database triggers
Dimensions
External procedure libraries
Index-organized tables
Indexes
Indextypes
Java classes, resources, and sources
Materialized views
Materialized view logs
Mining models
Object tables
Object types
Object views
Operators

Nonschema Objects
Contexts
Directories
Editions
Restore points
Roles
Rollback segments
Tablespaces
Users

Packages
Sequences
Stored functions and procedures
Synonyms
Tables
Views

Not all of the available object types will be referenced on the test. A list of the objects that you're likely to see on the test along with a brief definition follows:

- **TABLE** -- The basic structure to hold user data.
- **INDEX** -- A schema object that contains an entry for each value that appears in one or more columns of a table and provides direct, fast access to rows.
- **VIEW** -- A logical table based on one or more tables or views, although it contains no data itself.
- **SEQUENCE** -- A database object from which multiple users may generate unique integers.
- **SYNONYM** -- An alternative name for another object in the database.
- **CONSTRAINT** -- A rule that restricts the values in a database column.
- **USERS** -- An account through which database users can log in to the database and which provides the basis for creating schema objects.

Review the table structure

In relational databases, a table is a set of data elements organized using a model of vertical columns and horizontal rows. A table has a set number of columns, but can have any number of rows. When a table is created, the columns the will make up the table are defined. Column definitions will always contain at the bare minimum a data type. Additional aspects of the columns that may also be in the table definition include:

- Character fields are given a maximum size, and NUMBER fields can optionally be given a precision and scale. Most of the other fields such as DATE, LONG, and LOB data types do not have a defined maximum size.
- Columns definition can include constraints that restrict the data that is allowed in the column.
- Default values can be set for a column when rows are inserted without specifying a value.

The CREATE TABLE statement of Oracle has a dizzying number of options. In the SQL Fundamentals test you're required to know only a tiny fraction of the possible options. To create a table in Oracle, you must have the CREATE TABLE privilege and QUOTA on a tablespace that contains enough free space to hold the table you wish to create. At the very minimum for a table, you must specify a table name, and one column. The CREATE TABLE syntax for this is:

```
CREATE TABLE table_name (col1 datatype [, col2 datatype…]);

CREATE TABLE ocp_sample (
num_col     NUMBER,
nps_col     NUMBER(3,2),
chr_col     CHAR(10),
var_col     VARCHAR2(10),
dte_col     DATE);
```

In the example create statement above, two NUMBER fields are created (one with a defined precision and scale), one CHAR column, one VARCHAR, and one DATE. Only the character columns require a length to be specified. The precision and scale of a NUMBER column are optional. Unlike the values assigned to character data types, the precision and scale are not used to indicate the amount of space allocated for a NUMBER field but rather act as a constraint to limit the values allowed in it.

List the data types that are available for columns

Every value contained within the Oracle Database has a data type. The data type associates a given set of properties with the value and causes Oracle to treat the values differently. For example, It is possible to add, subtract, or multiply two values of the NUMBER data type, but not two values of a LONG data type. Any time a table is created, each of its columns must have a data type specified. Data types define the domain of values that each column can contain. There are a number of built-in data types in Oracle and it is possible to create user-defined types that can be used as data types. The data types available for columns are:

- **VARCHAR2(n)** -- Variable-length character string of n characters or bytes.
- **NVARCHAR2(n)** -- Variable-length Unicode character string of n characters.
- **NUMBER** -- Number having optional precision and scale values.
- **FLOAT** -- A subtype of the NUMBER data type having precision but no scale.
- **LONG** -- Character data of variable length up to 2 gigabytes.
- **DATE** -- This data type contains the datetime fields YEAR, MONTH, DAY, HOUR, MINUTE, and SECOND. It does not have fractional seconds or a time zone.
- **BINARY_FLOAT** -- 32-bit floating point number.
- **BINARY_DOUBLE** -- 64-bit floating point number.
- **TIMESTAMP** -- This data type contains the datetime fields YEAR, MONTH, DAY, HOUR, MINUTE, and SECOND. It contains fractional seconds but does not have a time zone.
- **TIMESTAMP WITH TIME ZONE** -- This data type contains the datetime fields YEAR, MONTH, DAY, HOUR, MINUTE, SECOND, TIMEZONE_HOUR, and TIMEZONE_MINUTE. It has fractional seconds and an explicit time zone.
- **TIMESTAMP WITH LOCAL TIME ZONE** – Identical to TIMESTAMP WITH TIME ZONE, with the exceptions that data is normalized to the database time zone when it is stored in the database, and displayed in the current session time zone when retrieved.
- **INTERVAL DAY TO SECOND** -- Stores a period of time in days, hours, minutes, and seconds
- **RAW(n)** -- Raw binary data of length n bytes.
- **LONG RAW** -- Raw binary data of variable length up to 2 gigabytes.
- **ROWID** -- Base 64 string representing the unique address of a row in its table.

- **UROWID** -- Base 64 string representing the logical address of a row of an index-organized table.
- **CHAR(n)** -- Fixed-length character data of length n bytes or characters.
- **NCHAR(n)** -- Fixed-length character data of length n characters.
- **CLOB** -- A character large object containing single-byte or multibyte characters.
- **NCLOB** -- A character large object containing Unicode characters.
- **BLOB** -- A binary large object.
- **BFILE** -- Contains a locator to a large binary file stored outside the database.

Large Object Columns

A LONG column is not, strictly speaking, a large object (LOB) column. However, it was the precursor to LOB data types. The LONG data type has several restrictions that LOB columns do not.

- Only one LONG column is allowed per table.
- They may not be included in GROUP BY or ORDER BY clauses.
- No constraints may be defined on a LONG column.

None of the LONG or LOB data types require (or allow) a size definition. LONG columns can contain up to 2 gigabytes of data. LOB columns and BFILES can contain up to 4 gigabytes.

Create a simple table

At its most basic, an Oracle create table statement would look something like the following:

```
CREATE TABLE ocp_example (
  ocp_id                NUMBER,
  ocp_name              VARCHAR2(20),
  ocp_date              DATE);
```

The statement can be broken down into the reserved words CREATE and TABLE, followed by a name for the table, and the column list. The column list must be enclosed in parentheses, and contain column name/data type pairs separated by commas. The table name and the column names must follow Oracle naming rules (discussed next). The SQL statement will be terminated by a semicolon.

Database Object Naming Rules

Every object in the database must have a name. The names may be represented with either a quoted identifier or a nonquoted identifier. A quoted identifier is enclosed in double quotation marks ("). A nonquoted identifier uses no punctuation. Quoted identifiers allow many of the Oracle database naming rules to be circumvented. However, Oracle does not recommend doing so. A complete list of the naming conventions is available in the Oracle SQL reference. A partial list follows:

- Names must be 1 to 30 bytes long with the exception of database names (8 bytes) and database links (128 bytes).
- Nonquoted identifiers cannot be Oracle SQL reserved words.
- Nonquoted identifiers must begin with an alphabetic character.
- Nonquoted identifiers can contain only alphanumeric characters from your database character set and the underscore (_), dollar sign ($), and pound sign (#).
- Nonquoted identifiers are not case sensitive. Oracle interprets them as uppercase. Quoted identifiers are case sensitive.
- Columns in the same table or view cannot have the same name. However, columns in different tables or views can have the same name.
- Within a namespace, no two objects can have the same name.

Namespaces

Namespaces are a construct that Oracle uses when locating a database object during the execution of a SQL command. In any single namespace, you may not have more than one object of the same. Each schema in the database has its own namespaces for the objects it contains.

The following schema objects share one namespace:
- Tables
- Views
- Sequences
- Private synonyms
- Stand-alone procedures
- Stand-alone stored functions
- Packages
- Materialized views
- User-defined types

The following schema objects each has its own namespace:
- Indexes
- Constraints
- Clusters
- Database triggers
- Private database links
- Dimensions

The upshot of this is that because tables and views are in the same namespace, you may not have a table and a view with the exact same name for a given schema. Likewise a table and a private synonym of the same name aren't allowed or a sequence and a view. However, indexes are in a separate namespace, so you could have a table and an index of the same name. In addition, because each schema has its own namespace, you could have tables of the same name in multiple schemas.

Altering a Table

Once a table has been created, any changes to its structure must be applied using the ALTER TABLE statement. Many of the options available during table creation can also be performed after it exists. The ALTER TABLE statement can be used to perform the following actions (among others – see the Oracle SQL Reference Guide for a complete list):

- Adding new columns
- Modifying existing column definitions
- Dropping existing columns
- Setting existing columns to UNUSED
- Renaming columns
- Adding or removing column constraints
- Adding default values to columns

Dropping a Table

If there is no longer a need for a table, you can use the DROP TABLE command to remove it from the data dictionary. By default, when a table is dropped in Oracle, it is not removed completely, but placed into a recycle bin. While the table is in the bin, it is possible to restore it. If you drop the table using the optional PURGE keyword, the table and its data will be dropped completely – bypassing the recycle bin. Until the table is purged from the recycle bin, no space is freed by the table drop and used space counts against the QUOTA for the owning user.

When a table is dropped, all objects dependent on it are invalidated (such as views and stored PL/SQL) and any indexes, constraints, and object privileges on the table are dropped.

Explain how constraints are created at the time of table creation

Constraints are database objects that are used to restrict (constrain) the data allowed into table columns. They are essentially rules that must be met in order for a value to be acceptable. There are several different kinds of constraints available in Oracle:

- **PRIMARY KEY** – The primary key of a table defines a column, or set of columns that must be unique for every row of a table. To satisfy a primary key constraint, none of the column(s) making up the key may be NULL, and the combination of values in the column(s) must be unique. A table can have only a single primary key constraint defined (all other constraint types can exist multiple times in the same table).
- **UNIQUE** – A unique key defines a column or set of columns that must be unique for every row of a table. Unlike a primary key constraint, the UNIQUE constraint does not prevent NULL values in the columns(s) comprising the constraint.
- **NOT NULL** – A NOT NULL constraint prevents a table column from having NULL values. If a column with a UNIQUE constraint is also defined as NOT NULL, it will have the same restrictive behavior as a PRIMARY KEY.
- **FOREIGN KEY** – Foreign keys are also referred to as Referential Integrity constraints. A foreign key constraint ties a column value in one table to a primary or unique key value in another. Values may not be inserted in the table with the reference constraint that do not exist in the referenced key.
- **CHECK** – Check constraints allow for custom conditions to be specified for a column. The conditions must evaluate to TRUE for the operation altering the column value to succeed.

Constraints in Oracle are created by one of two methods. They can be created simultaneously with the table during the CREATE TABLE statement, or they can be created on a table that already exists using the ALTER TABLE statement. There is no such thing as a 'CREATE CONSTRAINT' command. The SQL statement below creates a table with two constraints:

```
CREATE TABLE aircraft_types (
  act_id             NUMBER,
  act_name           VARCHAR2(20),
  act_body_style     VARCHAR2(10),
  act_decks          NUMBER,
  act_seats          NUMBER  NOT NULL
    CONSTRAINT ac_type_pk PRIMARY KEY (act_id)
);
```

Beyond creating the table and columns with associated data types, it contains the instructions for adding two constraints.

- The **act_seats** column has been assigned a NOT NULL constraint. If an insert to this table doesn't reference this column, or references it but attempts to add a NULL value to the column, an error will occur. Because no name was specified for the constraint, Oracle will give it a system-generated name. This is an in-line constraint definition because it is added in the same line as the column. NULL and NOT NULL constraints **must** be defined in-line during a CREATE or ALTER TABLE statements.
- The **act_id** column has been assigned a primary key constraint, and the constraint given the name 'ac_type_pk'. Oracle will create an index of the same name to enforce the primary key constraint. This constraint has been defined out-of-line.

The following is equivalent to the first SQL statement, with the primary key constraint being defined inline. The end result of a constraint defined in-line or out-of-line is identical.

```
CREATE TABLE aircraft_types (
  act_id             NUMBER  CONSTRAINT ac_type_pk
                             PRIMARY KEY,
  act_name           VARCHAR2(20),
  act_body_style     VARCHAR2(10),
  act_decks          NUMBER,
  act_seats          NUMBER  NOT NULL
);
```

It's possible to view these constraints by querying the USER_CONSTRAINTS view for all constraints associated with the AIRCRAFT_TYPES table. Note that the AC_TYPE_PK constraint is type P (Primary Key), and has no search condition. It is enforced by an index, not by a condition. By contrast the NOT NULL constraint is type 'C' (a NOT NULL constraint is in effect a specific type of check constraint), and has a condition that indicates the column should be NOT NULL.

```
SELECT constraint_name, constraint_type, search_condition
FROM   user_constraints
WHERE  table_name = 'AIRCRAFT_TYPES'

CONSTRAINT_NAME CONSTRAINT_TYPE SEARCH_CONDITION
--------------- --------------- -----------------------
AC_TYPE_PK      P
SYS_C007066     C               "ACT_SEATS" IS NOT NULL
```

Describe how schema objects work

Objects in the Oracle Database fall into two broad classes, schema objects and non-schema objects. If an object is associated with a particular schema, then it is a schema object. Conversely, if not, it is a non-schema object. A database schema is owned by and has the same name as an Oracle database user. The user and schema are not the same thing. However, since they are created simultaneously, cannot exist independently, and dropping a user drops the schema – the two are often treated as the same thing. The schema itself is defined as a collection of logical structures of data, or objects. Schema objects are created and manipulated via SQL statements. A partial list of schema objects follows:

- Constraints
- Database triggers
- Indexes
- Sequences
- Synonyms
- Tables
- Views

Nonschema Objects are also stored in the database and can be created and manipulated with SQL. However, they are not contained in a schema and (with the exception of users) have no affinity to any particular schema. A partial list of these includes:

- Directories
- Roles
- Rollback segments
- Tablespaces
- Users

Creating Other Schema Objects

In addition to tables, you'll need to recognize the syntax for creating views, sequences, indexes, and public synonyms. You'll also need to be familiar with what each of these objects is used for.

Create simple and complex views

A standard Oracle view is nothing more than a SQL statement that has been stored in the data dictionary. I'll note in passing that a Materialized View is *not* just a stored SQL statement. However, the two are not the same thing and materialized views are not a test topic. Once the SQL statement of a view has been stored in the data dictionary, it can be referenced as a logical table. It stores no data independent of the table it is based on. If the table is dropped, the view remains, but is invalid and will generate an error if queried. When a SQL query is performed against a view, what actually happens is that the Oracle SQL Parser combines the SQL of the view with the SQL of the query to make a single SQL statement against the base table(s) of the view.

Oracle differentiates views into two broad types, simple views and complex views. There is no distinction between the two from the standpoint of Oracle database objects. There is only one CREATE VIEW syntax. The difference lies in the operations present within the SELECT statements that define the view.

The base difference between simple and complex views is that a simple view selects from a single table and does not aggregate data or transform it via functions, whereas a complex view selects from more than one table and/or aggregates and/or transforms data. It is possible to perform DML operations against simple views. It **may** be possible to perform DML operations against a complex view, but it is dependent on the particular view.

You cannot delete or modify data via a view if either of the following is true:
- The view has aggregated data.
- The view contains the DISTINCT/UNIQUE keyword

You cannot insert data in a view if either of the above is true, or:
- There are NOT NULL columns in the table that are not selected by the view (unless these columns have a default value defined).

As a general rule you also cannot use DML on a query that contains JOINs. This rule can be circumvented if you have a key preserved table. However, key preserved tables are not an exam topic.

The following example is a simple view. It does not include the salary column from the EMPLOYEES table. Users given SELECT access on this view but *not* the base table will not be able to access employee salary information.

```
CREATE OR REPLACE VIEW employees_no_sal_v
AS
SELECT emp_first, emp_last, emp_job, start_date
FROM    employees;

view EMPLOYEES_NO_SAL_V created.
```

The OR REPLACE option in the CREATE VIEW syntax is optional. By including that option, if a view of that name already exists in the schema, it will be dropped and the current SQL syntax used to replace it. If the OR REPLACE option were left off and a view of that name already existed, the CREATE VIEW statement would fail with an error.

```
CREATE VIEW employees_no_sal_v
AS
SELECT emp_first, emp_last, emp_job, start_date
FROM    employees;

SQL Error: ORA-00955: name is already used by an existing
object
00955. 00000 -  "name is already used by an existing object"
*Cause:
*Action:
```

There are several other optional clauses that can be added to a CREATE VIEW statement:

- **FORCE** – Creates the view even if the base table(s) do not exist).
- **NOFORCE** – Only creates the view if the base tables exist (the default).
- **WITH CHECK OPTION** – Indicates that only rows accessible to the view can be inserted or updated.
- **WITH READ ONLY** – Specifies that no DML operations can be performed on the table through this view.

The following example is a complex view. By joining the AIRPORTS and AIRCRAFT_TYPES through the AIRCRAFT_FLEET table, this view allows you to easily query all of the aircraft in the fleet without having to create the joins each time.

```
CREATE OR REPLACE VIEW aircraft_fleet_v
AS
SELECT apt_name, apt_abbr, act_name, act_body_style,
act_decks, act_seats
FROM   airports apt
       INNER JOIN aircraft_fleet afl
       ON apt.apt_id = afl.apt_id
       INNER JOIN aircraft_types act
       ON act.act_id = afl.act_id;

view AIRCRAFT_FLEET_V created.
```

If any columns selected in the view are expressions, then the expression must be provided with an alias in order for a view to be created. The alias must meet normal naming convention rules. The following expands on the EMPLOYEE_NOSAL_V view created above, adding two new columns, one with the employee's full name separated by a space, and the second with their last name then the first name separated by a comma.

```
CREATE OR REPLACE VIEW employees_morenames_v
AS
SELECT emp_first, emp_last, emp_job, start_date,
       emp_first || ' ' || emp_last AS EMP_FULL_NAME,
       emp_last  || ', ' || emp_first AS EMP_LAST_FIRST
FROM   employees;

view EMPLOYEES_MORENAMES_V created.
```

An alternate syntax for defining the view column names during creation is:

```
CREATE OR REPLACE VIEW employees_morenames_v
    (emp_first, emp_last, emp_job, start_date,
     emp_full_name, emp_last_name)
AS
SELECT emp_first, emp_last, emp_job, start_date,
       emp_first || ' ' || emp_last,
       emp_last  || ', ' || emp_first
FROM   employees;

view EMPLOYEES_MORENAMES_V created.


DESCRIBE employees_morenames_v
Name            Null Type
-------------- ---- -------------
EMP_FIRST              VARCHAR2(10)
EMP_LAST              VARCHAR2(10)
EMP_JOB              VARCHAR2(10)
START_DATE            DATE
EMP_FULL_NAME        VARCHAR2(21)
EMP_LAST_FIRST       VARCHAR2(22)
```

In the example below, a view is created against the EMPLOYEES table using the WITH CHECK OPTION. The WHERE clause of the view restricts the rows returned by the query to those employees with 'Pilot' as their job title. The check option prevents any rows from being inserted via the view that would violate the WHERE condition (i.e. only pilots can be inserted).

```
CREATE OR REPLACE VIEW emp_pilots_v
AS
SELECT *
FROM    employees
WHERE   emp_job = 'Pilot'
WITH CHECK OPTION CONSTRAINT emp_pilot_ck;
```

```
SELECT emp_first, emp_last, emp_job, start_date
FROM   emp_pilots_v;

EMP_FIRST   EMP_LAST    EMP_JOB     START_DATE
----------  ----------  ----------  ----------
John        Jones       Pilot       10-APR-95
Top         Gun         Pilot       13-OCT-96
Phil        McCoy       Pilot       09-JUN-96
James       Thomas      Pilot       12-MAY-99
John        Picard      Pilot       11-NOV-01
Luke        Skytalker   Pilot       10-SEP-02
Dell        Aptop       Pilot       22-AUG-03
Noh         Kia         Pilot       07-JUL-04
```

Attempting to insert a manager into the view fails:

```
INSERT INTO emp_pilots_v VALUES (30, 9, 'Bo', 'String',
'Mgr', 10, 100000, '01-JAN-11');

SQL Error: ORA-01402: view WITH CHECK OPTION where-clause
violation
01402. 00000 -  "view WITH CHECK OPTION where-clause
violation"
*Cause:
*Action:
```

However, the same insert with 'Pilot' in the EMP_JOB column succeeds.

```
INSERT INTO emp_pilots_v VALUES (30, 9, 'Bo', 'String',
'Pilot', 10, 100000, '01-JAN-11');

1 rows inserted.
```

Creating a view using the WITH READ ONLY option prevents any DML from being issued against the table via the view:

```
CREATE VIEW emp_view_nodml_v
AS
SELECT *
FROM   employees
WITH READ ONLY;

SELECT emp_first, emp_last, emp_job, start_date
FROM   emp_view_nodml_v
WHERE  emp_job = 'Pilot';
```

```
EMP_FIRST    EMP_LAST     EMP_JOB     START_DATE
----------   ----------   ----------  ----------
John         Jones        Pilot       10-APR-95
Top          Gun          Pilot       13-OCT-96
Phil         McCoy        Pilot       09-JUN-96
James        Thomas       Pilot       12-MAY-99
John         Picard       Pilot       11-NOV-01
Luke         Skytalker    Pilot       10-SEP-02
Dell         Aptop        Pilot       22-AUG-03
Noh          Kia          Pilot       07-JUL-04

UPDATE  emp_view_nodml_v
SET     emp_last = 'Jones'
WHERE   emp_last = 'Kia';

SQL Error: ORA-42399: cannot perform a DML operation on a
read-only view
```

Retrieve data from views

Once a view exists, data is retrieved from it using SELECT statements just as if it were a table object. There are no changes to the SELECT syntax for queries against views rather than tables. It's not possible to determine from the results of a SELECT statement that the object being queried is a view rather than a table. Views are useful for a variety of purposes:

- **Reduce Complexity** -- A particularly complicated query of one or more tables in your database can be created as a view. Queries against the view then can be much simpler to create.
- **Reduce Maintenance** – Similar to the above -- if several parts of a database application will be querying one or more tables with the same basic SQL statement, creating a view that will support these queries will make maintenance easier if a change is required. Altering the view will propagate the changes to all of the SQL statements that use it.
- **Increase security** – If a table has some columns that can be accessed by one group of people and others that should not be, a view can be created without the columns on question. Access to query the view, but *not*the table can be granted to the group that should not see them.

```
SELECT emp_last_first, emp_full_name, emp_job
FROM    employees_morenames_v
ORDER BY emp_last_first;

EMP_LAST_FIRST          EMP_FULL_NAME          EMP_JOB
--------------------    ----------------------    ----------
Abong, Bill             Bill Abong             VP
Alien, Alf              Alf Alien              SrDir
Aptop, Dell             Dell Aptop             Pilot
Boss, Big               Big Boss               CEO
Gun, Top                Top Gun                Pilot
Jameson, Rick           Rick Jameson           SVP
Jeckson, Janet          Janet Jeckson          VP
Jones, John             John Jones             Pilot
Kia, Noh                Noh Kia                Pilot
McCoy, Phil             Phil McCoy             Pilot
Picard, John            John Picard            Pilot
Skytalker, Luke         Luke Skytalker         Pilot
Smith, Adam             Adam Smith             CFO
Stoneflint, Fred        Fred Stoneflint        SrDir
Stoner, Rob             Rob Stoner             SVP
Storm, Norm             Norm Storm             Mgr
Thomas, James           James Thomas           Pilot
```

Create, maintain, and use sequences

Sequences are database objects from which multiple users may generate
unique integers. They are often used to automatically generate primary
key values. Every time a sequence number is generated, the value is
incremented, <u>independent</u> of whether the transaction is committed or
rolled back. If a SQL statement generates an error, it is automatically
rolled back, but any sequences incremented by the call will **not** get rolled
back to the value they were previously.

One user can never acquire the sequence number that was generated by
another user. Once a sequence exists, the CURRVAL and NEXTVAL
pseudocolumns are used to access its values. The CURRVAL
pseudocolumn returns the current value of the sequence. The NEXTVAL
pseudocolumn increments the sequence and returns the new value. The
NEXTVAL and CURRVAL pseudocolumns cannot be used as part of a view,
or in an aggregate SELECT statement.

Since sequences do nothing more than return an integer when called, there are only a few questions to be answered when creating one and CREATE SEQUENCE is a fairly simple command:

START WITH – Specifies the first number to be returned by the sequence (default is 1).

INCREMENT BY – Specifies the integer that will be added to the sequence value each time it is called. This number can be positive or negative (default is 1).

MINVALUE – the lowest value that will be returned by the sequence (default is NOMAXVALUE).

MAXVALUE – The highest value that will be returned by the sequence (default is NOMINVALUE).

CYCLE – Sets the sequence will cycle through the same set of numbers continuously (START WITH to MINVALUE or MAXVALUE).

NOCYCLE – Sets the sequence to end when it hits the MAXVALUE or MINVALUE (the default).

CACHE – Determines whether or not the sequence will cache values in memory for faster retrieval and how many (default is CACHE 20).

NOCACHE – Disables caching for a sequence.

A sequence created with all default values will start at one, increment by 1 with no maximum value and utilize a cache of 20 values. To create a sequence that stops at a predefined limit, specify a value for the MAXVALUE or MINVALUE parameters (for ascending/descending sequences respectively) and add NOCYCLE. Once the sequence has reached its limit, any further calls to NEXTVAL generate an error.

To create a sequence that restarts after reaching a predefined limit, specify the MAXVALUE or MINVALUE parameter, and CYCLE. When a sequence is set to CYCLE, after the MAXVALUE (or MINVALUE) is reached, the next call to NEXTVAL will return the START WITH value.

The following example creates a sequence called SEQ_EMP_ID that starts with the number 18, increments by one each time the NEXTVAL pseudocolumn is referenced, and does not cache any values.

```
CREATE SEQUENCE seq_emp_id
START WITH 18
INCREMENT BY 1
NOCACHE;

sequence SEQ_EMP_ID created.
```

Once created, we can pull the next number from the sequence as follows:

```
SELECT seq_emp_id.nextval FROM dual;

NEXTVAL
-------
     18
```

If we were to make the above call a second time, it would return the value 19. However, we can pull the current sequence value without causing it to increment by usein thr CURRVAL pseudocolumn:

```
SELECT seq_emp_id.currval FROM dual;

CURRVAL
-------
     18
```

Where to use Sequence Values

You can use CURRVAL and NEXTVAL in the following locations:
- A SELECT list that is not part of a subquery, view, or materialized view.
- The SELECT list of a subquery used in an INSERT statement.
- The VALUES clause of an INSERT statement.
- The SET clause of an UPDATE statement.

You cannot use CURRVAL or NEXTVAL in the following locations:
- A subquery in an UPDATE, SELECT, or DELETE statement.
- A query of a view or materialized view.
- SELECT statements with DISTINCT, GROUP BY, or ORDER BY.
- A compound SELECT statement that uses SET operators.
- The WHERE clause of a SELECT.
- The DEFAULT value for a table.
- As part of a CHECK constraint condition

Gaps in sequences

Because the nature of sequences is to produce numbers at fixed increments, it is often assumed that using sequences to populate column data will never produce gaps in the data larger then the increment value. This is not the case. The two common events that can produce a gap in values produced by sequences are:

- **Caching** – When caching is enabled, the first time Oracle calls a sequence and no value is in memory, the database will grab the cache value of numbers (the default is 20), store these in memory, and immediately increment the sequence by the number cached in memory (i.e. 20). Subsequent calls to the sequence for NEXTVAL will not hit the sequence at all, but will return the values from cache until they are exhausted, at which point Oracle will grab another set and increment the sequence. If the database shuts down (normally or abnormally) while there are sequence numbers cached, they are 'lost'. The next time the database starts up, when the sequence is called, a new cache set will be pulled from the sequence and there will be a gap of however many numbers were in cache at the time of the shutdown.
- **Rollback** – If a SQL statement that calls NEXTVAL fails and is rolled back – the sequence number does not get rolled back. Likewise if one or more successful SQL statements are rolled back via the ROLLBACK command, any sequence numbers they generated are lost.

It's possible to use the ALTER SEQUENCE statement to change the INCREMENT, MINVALUE, MAXVALUE, CYCLE, or CACHE options of a sequence. It is not possible to change the START WITH value of a sequence using the ALTER TABLE command. The documentation notes that you must drop and recreate a sequence to change the START WITH value. That's not strictly true as there's a viable workaround, but for the purposes of the test, the answer to any question about changing the START WITH value is to drop and recreate the sequence.

Create and maintain indexes

Indexes are schema objects that store pointers to table rows based on data in the table. When the conditions of a query reference only columns that have no indexes, Oracle must scan every single row in the table (known as a full table scan). When indexes do exist on a queried column, Oracle has the option of using them and potentially speeding up data retrieval and reducing disk I/O. Creating or dropping indexes have no direct impact on the table. Dropping a table, however, will also drop any indexes created on the table.

Indexes contain an entry for each value that appears in the indexed column(s) of the table. Each index entry contains a locator to the block(s) in the data file containing the row(s) with that value and provide direct, fast access to them. It's possible to have multiple indexes on any given table. The tradeoffs involved in creating multiple indexes on the same table are outside the scope of this test. Any DML statement that includes an indexed column in a WHERE clause <u>might</u> see a performance benefit. The uncertainty lies in the fact that the Oracle Cost Based Optimizer may or may not choose to make use of the index.

Oracle supports several types of index:
- **Normal indexes** -- The default index type in Oracle is a B-tree index.
- **Bitmap indexes** -- Store the ROWID values associated with a key value as a bitmap. Bitmap indexes cannot be UNIQUE.
- **Partitioned indexes** -- Consist of partitions containing an entry for each value that appears in the indexed column(s) of the table.
- **Function-based indexes** – Store expressions based on column data rather than the column data itself. They enable you to construct queries that filter by an expression and get the performance benefit of an index.

When a primary key or unique constraint is added to a table, and there is not already an appropriate unique index on the column(s) the constraint is for, an index will be added to the table to enforce the constraint. We can find the index created earlier for the aircraft_types primary key by querying the USER_INDEXES view:

```
SELECT table_name, index_name
FROM   user_indexes
WHERE  table_name = 'AIRCRAFT_TYPES';

TABLE_NAME                   INDEX_NAME
------------------------     -------------
AIRCRAFT_TYPES               SYS_C006988
```

There are several rule-of-thumb guidelines on index creation. Indexing every column in every table is certainly not a good idea. Indexing no columns in any table is likewise generally not a good idea. Determining which columns to index in each table is the key to getting the best performance boost possible from indexing.

Signs that you might want an index built on a column:
- The column has a broad range of values.
- The table is large and queries tend to retrieve less than 2-4% of the table rows.
- The column is often used in a WHERE clause or as a JOIN column.
- The column contains a large number of NULL values.

Signs that you might NOT want an index built on a column:
- The column is seldom used as a query condition or JOIN column.
- The table is frequently updated.
- The table is small or most queries return more than 2-4% of the table rows.
- The columns are generally referenced as part of an expression.

When creating indexes manually via the CREATE INDEX command, you can index a single column:

```
CREATE INDEX emp_last_ndx
ON employees (emp_last);

index EMP_LAST_NDX created.
```

You can also create an index that contains multiple columns:

```
CREATE INDEX emp_last_first_ndx
ON employees (emp_last, emp_first);

index EMP_LAST_FIRST_NDX created.
```

You can view information about the indexes on a table in the USER_INDEXES view.

```
SELECT index_name, index_type, uniqueness
FROM   user_indexes
WHERE  table_name = 'EMPLOYEES';

INDEX_NAME                INDEX_TYPE      UNIQUENESS
--------------------      --------------  ----------
EMP_LAST_FIRST_NDX        NORMAL          NONUNIQUE
EMP_LAST_NDX              NORMAL          NONUNIQUE
SYS_C006990               NORMAL          UNIQUE
```

Whenever a DML query includes one or more indexed columns in the WHERE clause, the Oracle Cost Based Optimizer has to decide whether or not making use of the index will improve the performance of the operation. The optimizer uses table statistics to try to determine what percentage of rows in the table will be returned by the query. If the answer is most (or all) of the rows in the table, then skipping the index in favor of a full-table scan is likely to be the better option from a performance standpoint. The full scope of the CBO decision-making process is much more complex, but this is a significant part of the decision on using indexes. Indexes are never used when the comparison being performed is '!=', 'NOT IN', or 'IS NULL' or if the column being compared is in a function and the index is not a function-based index (using the same function as is in the WHERE clause).

Oracle maintains indexes automatically. There is no command that you must issue to account for a row being added or deleted, or an indexed value being changed. Every time a table change is made that affects an indexed value, Oracle performs the necessary changes to all affected indexes on that table. The automated work is part of the downside to having multiple indexes on a given table. Multiple indexes **might** improve performance for selects, but they **will** create overhead that reduces performance for inserts, updates and deletes.

The only manual performance operation that you might perform on an index is a rebuild. Index rebuilds can sometimes reduce the size and improve the performance characteristics for an index that has had a lot of data changes since the index was built (or last rebuilt).

```
ALTER INDEX emp_last_first_ndx REBUILD;

index EMP_LAST_FIRST_NDX altered.
```

If you decide that an index is not being used or if you want to replace it with an index created in a different fashion, you can remove it from the data dictionary with the DROP INDEX command. If a table with indexes is dropped, all of the associated indexes will be dropped automatically.

```
DROP INDEX emp_last_first_ndx;

index EMP_LAST_FIRST_NDX dropped.
```

Create private and public synonyms

A SYNONYM in Oracle is a data dictionary object that is an alternate name for a different data dictionary object. It has **no** connection to the object that it points to, and indeed a SYNONYM can be created for a non-existent object. If an object that a synonym points to is dropped, the synonym itself is unchanged (and the reverse is true as well).

SYNONYMs are useful for separating the fully-qualified names of databases objects from the names used to reference them in database applications. For example, assume you had a developer who created an application in the schema JJONES with all tables, procedures, etc. in there. If he left the company, moving those objects out of the schema would likely require a significant amount of development to point everything to their new location. SYNONYMS can be used to either prevent problems like this from occurring or solve them after the fact.

There are two broad classes of synonyms:

- **PRIVATE** – Private synonyms are schema objects. They are used only for calls that originate in the schema in which they are created.
- **PUBLIC** – Public synonyms are non-schema objects. They are available to all database users.

Once a synonym exists, it can be used as part of a SQL statement. As mentioned above, the synonym doesn't verify the destination object exists or provide any rights to it if it does. If a SELECT statement against the base table will fail, then a SELECT statement against a synonym referencing it will fail as well. All that really happens inside Oracle when a synonym is used is that Oracle replaces one identifier with the other before executing the SQL. In the below example, a private synonym named VIEW_EMPLOYEES is created for the EMPLOYEES_MORENAMES_V view.

```
CREATE OR REPLACE SYNONYM view_employees FOR
employees_morenames_v;

synonym VIEW_EMPLOYEES created.
```

Executing a DESCRIBE against the new synonym shows the structure of the EMPLOYEES_MORENAMES_V view.

```
DESC view_employees

Name            Null Type
-------------- ---- ------------
EMP_FIRST            VARCHAR2(10)
EMP_LAST             VARCHAR2(10)
EMP_JOB              VARCHAR2(10)
START_DATE           DATE
EMP_FULL_NAME        VARCHAR2(21)
EMP_LAST_FIRST       VARCHAR2(22)
```

In the below example, a public synonym named VIEW_EMPLOYEES is created for the EMPLOYEES_NO_SAL_V view.

```
CREATE OR REPLACE PUBLIC SYNONYM view_employees FOR
employees_no_sal_v;

public synonym VIEW_EMPLOYEES created.
```

The statement succeeds even though a private synonym of that name already exists. This is because public and private synonyms don't share the same namespace. Executing a DESCRIBE against the new synonym still shows the structure of the EMPLOYEES_MORENAMES_V view, however.

```
DESC view_employees
Name            Null Type
-------------- ---- ------------
EMP_FIRST            VARCHAR2(10)
EMP_LAST            VARCHAR2(10)
EMP_JOB            VARCHAR2(10)
START_DATE          DATE
EMP_FULL_NAME      VARCHAR2(21)
EMP_LAST_FIRST    VARCHAR2(22)
```

This is because when Oracle is resolving an object, it will look in the current schema first. If you have a private synonym named VIEW_EMPLOYEES in your schema pointing to object A, and there is a public synonym named VIEW_EMPLOYEES that points to object B, then a query from inside your schema against the name VIEW_EMPLOYEES will pull results from object A. If the private synonym created earlier is dropped, then executing a DESCRIBE against the VIEW_EMPLOYEES will show the structure of the EMPLOYEES_NO_SAL_V view.

```
DROP SYNONYM view_employees;

synonym VIEW_EMPLOYEES dropped.

DESC view_employees

Name        Null Type
---------- ---- ------------
EMP_FIRST        VARCHAR2(10)
EMP_LAST        VARCHAR2(10)
EMP_JOB        VARCHAR2(10)
START_DATE      DATE
```

The syntax to DROP a private synonym follows. If you are not the owner of the synonym, you must prefix it with a schema name.

```
DROP SYNONYM view_employees;
```

The syntax to DROP a public synonym follows. PUBLIC synonyms are not associated with a schema and will never have a schema prefix. The keyword PUBLIC is the only way to reference a public synonym to drop it.

```
DROP PUBLIC SYNONYM view_employees;
```

Schema References

When performing DML operations against objects that exist in the current schema, the object name is sufficient for Oracle to locate it and execute the operation against it. However, when an object exists in another schema, the object name must be prefixed by the schema name. For example, the departments table exists in the HR schema on the system used in creating this guide. Selecting from this table without a schema reference generates an error:

```
SELECT *
FROM    departments
WHERE   department_id < 70;

ORA-00942: table or view does not exist
00942. 00000 -  "table or view does not exist"
```

If the table name is prefixed by the schema name and a period, the SELECT operation succeeds:

```
SELECT *
FROM    hr.departments
WHERE   department_id < 70;
```

DEPARTMENT_ID	DEPARTMENT_NAME	MANAGER_ID	LOCATION_ID
10	Administration	200	1700
20	Marketing	201	1800
30	Purchasing	114	1700
40	Human Resources	203	2400
50	Shipping	121	1500
60	IT	103	1400

Resolving schema names invisibly is one of the most common uses of
synonyms, both private and public. Creating a synonym called
DEPARTMENTS for HR.DEPARTMENTS eliminates the need to qualify the
schema when querying the table.

```
CREATE SYNONYM departments FOR hr.departments;

SELECT *
FROM    departments
WHERE   department_id < 70;

synonym DEPARTMENTS created.
DEPARTMENT_ID DEPARTMENT_NAME     MANAGER_ID LOCATION_ID
------------- ------------------- ---------- -----------
           10 Administration      200        1700
           20 Marketing           201        1800
           30 Purchasing          114        1700
           40 Human Resources     203        2400
           50 Shipping            121        1500
           60 IT                  103        1400
```

ABOUT THE AUTHOR

Matthew Morris has worked with the Oracle database since 1996 when he worked in the RDBMS support team for Oracle Support Services. Employed by Oracle for over eleven years in support and development positions, Matthew was an early adopter of the Oracle Certified Professional program. He was one of the first one hundred Oracle Certified Database Administrators (version 7.3) and was also in the first hundred to become an Oracle Certified Forms Developer. In the years since, he has upgraded his Database Administrator certification for releases 8i, 9i, 10G and 11G, and added the Application Express Expert and the Oracle SQL Expert certifications. Outside of Oracle, he has CompTIA certifications in Linux+ and Security+.

Matthew is an experienced Database Administrator and PL/SQL developer and has been creating Web applications with Oracle Application Express since the early days of its release. He is currently employed as a Database Engineer with Computer Sciences Corporation developing enterprise applications.

Made in the USA
Lexington, KY
08 October 2013